WORK AND PEACE IN ACADEME

WORK AND PEACE IN ACADEME

Leveraging Time, Money, and
Intellectual Energy
Through Managing Conflict

James R. Coffman
Kansas State University

ANKER PUBLISHING COMPANY, INC.
Bolton, Massachusetts

WORK AND PEACE IN ACADEME
Leveraging Time, Money, and Intellectual Energy Through Managing Conflict

ISBN 1-882982-84-3

Composition by Beverly Jorgensen, Studio J Graphic Design
Cover design by Knoll Gilbert

Anker Publishing Company, Inc.
563 Main Street
P.O. Box 249
Bolton, MA 01740-0249 USA

www.ankerpub.com

Library of Congress Cataloging-in-Publication Data

Coffman, James R.
  Work and peace in academe : leveraging time, money, and intellectual energy through managing conflict / James R. Coffman.
      p. cm.
  Includes bibliographical references and index.
  ISBN 1-882982-84-3
  1. College personnel management. 2. Conflict management. 3. Communication in education. 4. Universities and colleges—Administration. I. Title.

  LB2331.66.C64 2005
  378.1'1—dc22
                        2005004601

To my family.

TABLE OF CONTENTS

About the Author

James R. Coffman has had a diversified career, which contributed substantially to his interest in and views about dealing with conflict in the academic environment. He served as head of the Department of Veterinary Surgery and Medicine and as dean of the College of Veterinary Medicine before being appointed provost at Kansas State University in 1987. He served as provost for 17 years before stepping down in June of 2004. Early in his career, Coffman was in private veterinary medical practice. He also served on the Veterinary Clinical Sciences faculty at Kansas State University and the University of Missouri, specializing in equine medicine. He published more than 100 scientific and professional papers and one book in his discipline and lectured widely in the United States and internationally. He served as president of the American Association of Equine Practitioners, which includes members from more than 40 countries, as well as president of the American College of Internal Veterinary Medicine. While dean of the College of Veterinary Medicine, Coffman chaired a gubernatorial task force that drafted the legislation for pari-mutuel wagering in Kansas. He also served on the American Veterinary Medical Association's Professional Liability Insurance Trust, including two years as chairman. Coffman chaired a National Research Council Board on Agriculture subcommittee on the use of drugs in food producing animals. He has extensive experience in policy development in postsecondary education at the university level and through service on the Council of Chief Academic Officers of the

Kansas Board of Regents universities. Coffman served on the Council on Academic Affairs Executive Committee in the National Association of State Universities and Land-Grant Colleges and on an American Council on Education-sponsored task force on development of academic policy, which included multiple categories of institutions.

As a chief academic officer for 17 years, Coffman developed an ever greater interest in the prevention, resolution, and management of unproductive conflict, recognizing the injurious effect on individuals and the very large attendant loss of human and financial resources to the institution. These interests included extensive involvement in and furtherance of success for women and people of color, as well as conflict related to race and gender. He worked with faculty, staff, and other administrators to develop and refine policies and procedures to deal with conflict by addressing its causes and effects. This included policy facilitating the individualization of faculty work, along with improved approaches to post-tenure review, appeal, grievance, affirmative action, and alternative means of dispute resolution. This effort came to include creation of an institution-level, integrated systematic approach to resolution of disputes that preserved the value of productive conflict and the importance of informal methods.

Coffman's background includes immediate family members who were or are attorneys. One of these was his father and the other is one of his sons. This, coupled with experience in private veterinary medical (equine) practice, fourteen years as a faculty member, three years as head of a large academic department, three years as a dean, leadership roles in large, complex state and national organizations and projects, and seventeen years as the chief academic officer of a land-grant university, comprises a body of experience that is unique and affords a fresh look at how to evaluate and address conflict in the academic environment.

Acknowledgments

Were it not for the insight and advice of my colleagues at Kansas State University, I would not have been able to conceptualize this work. This includes the central administration, the deans and department heads and chairs, the faculty, and faculty governance and administrative officers in many areas relevant to the subject matter, including the university attorneys.

I especially appreciate the dedicated work of what came to be called The Dispute Resolution Group at Kansas State University. Their commitment to improving the resolution of disputes of all kinds, and the innovation and ability they brought to their work, had substantial influence on my thinking and personal growth.

Special thanks to Mr. Daniel Reveles of Tecate, Mexico, for his critique of this and other work, and for helping me learn to write serviceable dialogue.

INTRODUCTION

My father was a county seat lawyer in a town of 700. He favored property law and planning for estate tax avoidance over litigation and sent most people seeking divorce home to think it over. I learned some valuable things from him about conflict prevention and resolution. More than once, he told me that the main value of a contract is to define how an arrangement will be dissolved in an orderly manner if it doesn't work out. The point was that if the project under contract is going to work, it depends on the quality of the concept, the level of performance by the parties, and the chemistry between them. If one of these elements fails, then a clear set of rules is needed for orderly resolution or dissolution. This underscores the importance of having a predetermined means of addressing differences.

Of great practical value was my father's suggestion that when writing a letter that is likely to have an inflammatory effect, it is best to show the receiving party a draft before you send it. This is a sign of respect; it sets the other party to thinking about the problem from a different perspective and often results in identifying one or more points of resolution. Letters take on a life of their own, committing the elements of a dispute to posterity along with the hard feelings that accompany them. It is, of course, 180 degrees away from the memo exchange that often hardens warring factions into irreconcilable differences.

I started my own career as a veterinarian in private equine practice. It should be understood here that while horses were the object of work and I love them very much as a species and in some instances as individuals, veterinary medicine, like most career pursuits, is far more about people than animals. It also is predicated on good diagnosis. I have found that the diagnostic (fact finding) process, regard for people, and accountability that were necessary aspects of my first horse practice are essential ingredients in dispute resolution. If everyone on a college or university campus treated each other with the respect my clients expected from me, most of the disputes we encounter would not happen in the first place.

It also was the case, however, that if I did not feel comfortable doing work for a client, I could decline to do so once a specific responsibility had been discharged. Conversely, if a client did not like me or the services I rendered, she simply called someone else the next time she needed help. Either party could dissolve the relationship painlessly.

I have served as an officer, board member, or trustee in a number of large, national professional organizations. In such instances, officers and board members meet several times a year, and when their term is served they go on to something else. They are not closely associated year in and year out, rubbing personalities every day and dependent on each other for long-term success. It becomes clear that disassociation is a ready option, even a built-in characteristic of many professional arrangements. Not so in academic settings. Department faculty in colleges and universities are bound together in much tighter fashion. The bonds of coinvestigators and coauthors, kids in school, spousal employment, and tenure create an imperative of continuity that is, to some extent, unique. This is especially so when state budgets across the country run low (a modern norm) and academic employment alternatives are limited.

Thus, the basic premise of this book is that colleges and universities possess distinctive characteristics that have important implications for dispute prevention, resolution, and management (DPRM). This is so to a greater degree in institutions with tenure, especially in those with multiple aspects to the mission; for example, teaching, research and service in contrast to teaching only. Within the basic rubric of post-secondary education institutions, each one has its own history, culture, and tradition that is unique and of powerful importance in developing a system of DPRM.

GOVERNING POLICIES, PROCEDURES, AND PRACTICES

In contrast to the private sector, public institutions are bound to all the employment laws and regulations specific to the public sector of the state in which the institution resides, as well as all other state and federal laws and regulations that apply to all of education and business. Public and private research universities also receive funding from federal agencies and are subject to additional federal regulations, such as the Bahye-Dole act governing the disposition of intellectual property derived from federally funded research.

The post-World War II emergence of research universities as a major part of the country's research and development effort has made intellectual property, patents, and copyright a large new field within which the seeds of conflict can and will germinate. If a faculty member in the English department invents a new kind of mousetrap in his basement at home, he owns the patent outright. If a chemistry professor invents a new compound in a university laboratory, using university technical assistance and equipment funded by a federal grant, the resultant intellectual property belongs to the institution. Everything in between may be subject to definition and, therefore, to disagreement and misunderstanding. The potential for conflict is greater in the area of copyright than patents because ownership is more difficult to establish and mediated instruction and distance-learning revenues (which are heavily dependent upon copyrighted material) place the dispute at the heart of the institutional mission and revenue base.

Colleges and universities, and individual departments within them, commonly have something akin to a faculty handbook containing all of the institution's policies and prescribed procedures. In many if not most instances, the handbook has the force of a contract. However, it often lacks clarity, both at the institutional level and at the individual level. These documents can become garbled and out of date. The contents are developed and continuously revised through an iterative ebb and flow between the faculty governance, administration, and bargaining unit, if one exists. While this very process can be a source of conflict, issues as to which version is current and how the wording is to be interpreted by subsequent users create innumerable possibilities for misunderstanding when applied to individual cases.

This constellation of laws, regulations, policies, procedures, and practices impacting public and private nonprofit institutions is unique. It comprises a body of canon and civil law. Colleges and universities are closer to the church than to the business community in this way. They operate within an environment in which certain basic principles prevail. One of the most important is academic freedom. The concept of academic freedom carries the implication (and in most instances the reality) that the members of the academic community have an unusual degree of autonomy in the conduct of their work and virtually unlimited freedom of expression, both in their area of scholarship and in their elaboration of views on any issue. The scope of potential situations pertaining to academic freedom expands as the mission of the institution increases and diversifies from a teaching only two-year institution to a multifaceted doctoral-granting research university.

ACADEMIC FREEDOM, ACCOUNTABILITY, COLLEGIALITY, AND CIVILITY

Linked to the idea of academic freedom are issues of accountability, collegiality, and civility. The balance between accountability and individual academic freedom can be a source of conflict between faculty members and, more often, between an individual faculty member and an administrator, the first in line being the department head or chair. Resultant disputes might range from a real or perceived lack of productivity to controversial public statements to disagreements about pedagogy to areas of research interest that do not pertain to the mission of the academic unit. The list is virtually infinite; the factors mentioned here are merely some of the most common.

Likewise, the balance between academic freedom and collegiality is fertile ground for the seeds of conflict. Language is an issue here. In daily conversation, the term *collegiality* is commonly used interchangeably with *civility*—an important departure from the dictionary definition of shared authority. Collegiality even finds its way into promotion and tenure decision-making in an attempt to increase the likelihood that a newly tenured colleague will be a good department citizen for the balance of his employment. At Kansas State University, where I spent the majority of my administrative career, departments that used collegiality as a criterion for tenure and promotion were required by policy to define it in terms specific to that unit. *Civility* is a better word when behavior is the issue. When the point of collegiality really is shared power or authority, that issue alone can be a source of conflict, be it in the balance of power among faculty in a department or between faculty governance and the administration, the deans and the provost, or the president and the governing board.

Thus, issues pertaining to collegiality and civility are legion in college and university environments. Raw debate and serious disagreement on such issues as policy, pedagogy, curriculum, and research are essential to the academic process. However, the need for such exchange, under the label of academic freedom, can become a paper tiger behind which outright uncivil or abusive behavior or chronic disruption of reasoned procedures can hide. While the loyal curmudgeon may play a valuable role, the chronically condescending, confrontational, or threatening individual may simply be a source of stress and lost productivity for other people. The difference between the two is that the former goes after ideas, albeit in a crusty and sometimes confrontational manner; the latter goes after people, albeit in subtle and sometimes arcane ways. Interestingly, since colleges and universities are places where ideas, points of view, ideologies, and academic freedom are cornerstones, many of its citizens are apt to think that, by definition, interpersonal conflict is not a major or even significant problem.

One of the subtle inconsistencies in the academic freedom milieu is that tenure-track faculty, who will be voted on by tenured faculty as part of the tenure granting process, can be reluctant to voice their views or take on the establishment for fear of getting crosswise with someone who will help to decide their fate. Usually this is unfounded, but perception can take on the force of reality in such circumstances. This problem is made much worse by lack of clear criteria, standards, policies, and procedures for annual evaluation, promotion, and tenure. Conflict is sure to arise in such an environment and can persist in perpetuity because the warring parties often are bound together by the intended permanence of tenure. Tenure, and to some extent promotion, is the most frequent source of serious conflict involving individual people at institutions which offer it.

Tenure, with all its virtues, can contribute to an environment that leads to conflict. Most disputes involve individuals or groups who are, in most instances, going to continue working together in an academic unit. It is vitally important to the entire institution whether they resolve their differences constructively or continue their dispute with its resultant emotional and intellectual drain, loss of productivity, and compromised career advancement.

In most instances, conflict in an academic environment requires only a clear pathway along which to pursue resolution. On occasion, however, a stream of disputes develops around an individual who does not truly seek resolution but instead displays an apparent desire to maintain an atmosphere of conflict with him at its epicenter. A first cousin to this individual is the person who cannot resist fanning any flame he finds. When fires break out these rare individuals always seem to be standing in the shadows with an empty gasoline can. An effective system of DPRM must account for each set of circumstances.

ADMINISTRATION AND GOVERNANCE

The collegial relationship between the faculty leadership and the administration is unique to academe. It can be the classic double-edged sword: a major source of conflict or one of the institution's most powerful instruments of dispute prevention and resolution. The administration has primary responsibility for policy implementation and budget management. The faculty has primary responsibility for the curriculum and the conduct of their research. Everything in between is negotiable and, to a great extent, subject to the role of the governing board, the history and culture of the institution, and the personality and style of the players. Faculty leadership is elected annually, so those personalities and styles change frequently, a situation often compounded by rapid turnover of administrators, especially deans, chief academic officers, and presidents.

Thus professional development and training of administrators at every level in matters pertinent to DPRM is extremely important. Such programs are increasing in number, especially for department heads and chairs. These programs often address how to deal with people in difficult situations and some address interpersonal style. If done well, there is a salutary effect on the well-being of the institution and on the careers of affected administrators, faculty, and staff.

Dealing constructively with conflict is one of the most important aspects of any administrator's responsibilities. All too often, the pressure conflict creates impacts the person to the extent that she avoids it and is thus rendered ineffective. In others, inability to cope with the resultant stress affects the individual's health and may drive him out of an administrative career. However, when people can view dealing with conflict as a desirable, thorough-going, fact-finding process couched in terms of basic fairness, they then can deal with it as an intellectual exercise, be fair and effective, and experience far less stress. Professionals in the field call this *depersonalizing conflict*. Having begun my career in equine veterinary medicine, I view it as a diagnostic process implemented through good people skills.

THE IMPORTANCE OF COMMUNICATION

The distribution and clarification of information about circumstances and events impacting the institution is a major factor in prevention of disputes. The most common criticism of administrators by faculty is lack of communication. They believe that the more transparent the institutional priorities and fiscal conditions are to the faculty and staff, the better. They are right. There are times when maximum, intensive efforts must be made to communicate as much information as feasible to as many people as possible. Examples include fiscal crises and attacks on tenure by regents or state government. In public institutions, this state of affairs reaches an annual high point when the legislature is in session. Furthermore, the legislature usually is in session during the second half of the academic year when institutional nerves already are frayed. Suspicion runs hot among the uninformed, along with resentment about being kept in the dark. This kind of background noise produces an environment of discontent where conflict prospers and disputes flourish.

Fragmented information and statements out of context generate rumors at a ferocious pace, which raises an interesting point about the academic persona. Faculty members are meticulous about fact-finding and accuracy in their discipline-based research and teaching. No successful scholar would consider publishing a paper that she did not believe was thoroughly researched, documented, and accurate. This basic premise is often thrown out the window, however, when the rumor mill is humming, resulting in hallway speculation and gossip that can consume time and intellectual energy. Conflict sprouts like mushroom spores under these conditions.

It can never be assumed that an appeal and grievance system and a means of investigating claims of discrimination and harassment are adequate. They are not. For example, because an affirmative action claim does not rise to the level of the legal standard for discrimination, it cannot be assumed that a problem does not exist. There must be avenues available for referral through which the underlying issues can be addressed if working relationships are to be preserved or recovered. These same mechanisms can be brought into play to nip problems in the bud before they reach the formal complaint, appeal, or grievance stage. This does not mean that every problem can be resolved to everyone's satisfaction. But it does mean that misunderstandings can be corrected before they become something greater.

These circumstances, many of which are limited to the academy, underscore the importance of institutional policies, procedures, and practices that include a clear, well-understood, and user-friendly system of DPRM that is part of the culture and not subject to the continual coming and going of specific people.

CONCLUSION

The purpose of this book is to assess the nature of conflict in academic environments and describe practical ways to prevent and resolve unproductive disputes. At the same time, it emphasizes the need to retain the value of productive conflict. It is predicated on the reality that every institution of higher education is different in terms of history, culture, policy, practice, and mission. To effectively develop a systemic approach to dispute prevention, resolution, and management that preserves informal resolution, these factors must be taken into account. The foundation stones of integrity and trust are cited throughout as critical to the ongoing success of any system or approach.

This book contains many stories and vignettes, including four example cases at the end, aimed at integrating the basic ideas and emphasizing the importance of innumerable nuances attendant to resolving conflict. Except for two stories that clearly are historical, and one scenario based partially on a mistake of my own making, all of these accounts are complete fiction.

1 ◆ CONFLICT: TWO SIDES OF ONE COIN

The term *unproductive conflict* implies the existence of productive conflict. In fact, conflict plays an essential role in any organization, including colleges and universities. The following discussion explores the cost of unproductive conflict, why it is so essential to minimize it, and the nature of productive conflict and its importance in the long-term well-being of the institution.

UNPRODUCTIVE CONFLICT

Academe is a place of ideas, whether the institution is a community college, a small liberal arts college, a master's level comprehensive university, or a large research university. The free exchange of information and knowledge is central to the existence of the institution. This is just as true in the classroom as it is in the research laboratory. Ideas, information, and knowledge abound in every academic discipline and are subject to change every hour of every day.

Disputes about ideas and the validity of information and knowledge are part of everyday academic life. The discourse can be interesting, even fun. The more this happens in the classroom, the better; this is the fertile loam in which the seeds of active learning are best planted. It is this very discourse that kept the press and wishful thinking from stampeding the country into accepting too quickly the idea of cold fusion. The unrelenting investigation of Piltdown man finally revealed the hoax, allowed to persist for decades by the ebb and flow between the British Museum and academe. The list of such instances is endless, notably marked by Darwin's discourse with his inner self along his sand path or Watson and Crick critiquing the direction of their research in their laboratory office.

However, ideas and information, even received wisdom, have a way of becoming identified with individual people and their careers. Thus, it is predictable that the discourse will, with some frequency, shift to the people behind the ideas rather than the ideas themselves. Lifelong disputes may then develop. This is tolerable when the disputants are far removed from one another. When they are in the same academic department, the negative impact on themselves, their immediate colleagues, and their institution can be devastating. Real instances have occurred where two antagonistic faculty members of long-standing prominence have maintained wars and warring factions that finally led to the dissolution of their department. Worse still, average and below average individuals can create a level of chronic inflammation sufficient to disrupt a unit to the point of damaging the careers of those around them, hurting their institution in the process. Most egregious, they inflict stress, strain, and poor quality of instruction on the students in their charge. This behavior should never be allowed to proceed once detected, and it can be resolved or managed in the large majority of instances. Better yet, much of it can be prevented.

Such unproductive conflict drains away the only thing the institution really has to offer: intellectual resources and the energy to elaborate them. Time and intellectual energy spent in retreat behind closed doors, hallway gossip, and general commiseration is time not invested in the scholarship of discovery, teaching and learning, integration, and application. Students are shortchanged, careers are impeded, and the institution loses ground. Anguish prevails where a little joy would do nicely. The worst of it is that these losses are very real, and they never can be recovered. Never!

Unproductive conflict is common in governance matters as well. Conflict and disputes are necessary in developing sound policy to further the future of the institution and the people in it. This ebb and flow works as long as a general sense of trust exists among the parties and the debate stays focused on the issues rather than the people around them. However, if the administration makes misleading statements, albeit intentionally or inadvertently, about the budget or some other high-profile issue of the day, uncertainty about the people behind those statements begins to take precedence over resolution of the issues themselves. This creates an environment where those rare individuals who thrive on conflict can rise to their full potential. This might be achieved through bombastic statements in the faculty assembly or disinformation attached to fragments of truth disseminated through innumerable ingenious means. Email has armed these people to the teeth, especially those who have mastered the art and science of the mass electronic mailing of anonymous messages. The very real potential for such conflicted events to get out of hand and throw the institution into a state of chronic or acute turmoil underscores the essential nature of honest dealing, good communication (there can never be enough), mutual respect, and a policy and process that are followed.

In more prosaic terms, unproductive conflict has a very real fiscal impact. The lion's share of the budget of most academic units is devoted to salaries and fringe benefits. When the cost of the kind of conflict just described is translated into actual time of faculty, staff, and administration, large sums of money are wiped away daily, not including lost grants and contracts, unbestowed endowments, and, in the case of public universities, withheld legislative funding due to the appearance that the institution is in disarray.

Henry Kissinger's oft-quoted statement to the effect that politics are so rife in universities because the stakes are so low has it dead wrong. The stakes are very high. Beyond the importance of research and service, consider the number of students enrolling in higher education in the United States, then consider the impact they will have on the future course of the country. The students and their future impact raise the stakes very high.

PRODUCTIVE CONFLICT

In an academic environment, productive conflict can be presented in two forms: conflict about ideas and conflict about people and their performance. It would be easy to add conflict about money, but resource issues are important only as they relate to people and their productive performance.

CONFLICT ABOUT IDEAS

Ideas drive society in general and academic institutions in particular. In research universities, the pool of ideas covers a bigger and more speculative front. Intellectual exploration is a strong characteristic of most people who find their way into an academic career. Those who are most successful are driven by it. When this spark burns out, careers plateau, and if this becomes endemic, the institution goes downhill. This is just as true for small liberal arts colleges or community colleges as it is for comprehensive regional institutions and large research universities.

The exchange of ideas and points of view about ideas ranges from governance issues and campus politics to fine points of aesthetic discernment, to string theory, molecular biology, Greek literature, and everything in between. This is the yeast that makes the dough rise. Teaching and learning in this environment can take students to a much higher level in terms of lifelong intellectual aspirations than it would in a mere exchange of information. God forbid that the members of an academic community ever agree on something all at the same time. The institution would implode.

The interaction intrinsic in conflict about ideas and academic tradition creates many an interesting paradox. Traditional colleges and universities are assumed to last forever. This is why donors give money to them and why alumni look forward to their children and grandchildren attending their alma mater. It also has a lot to do with why institutional change comes so slowly and with such great agonizing. This, of course, frustrates no-nonsense people in the private sector who think the university ought to run like a business. Business executives and middle management do not parade through corporate headquarters in black gowns and colorful regalia two or three times a year to reinforce the importance of core values that go back 900 years. Academic administrators and faculty do. It is paradoxical that in those same archaic institutions, a great deal of the world's intellectual advancement and new knowledge comes into being. The basic science that will drive the technology of the future is advanced there, just as it is in the research and development operations of private business. This internal paradox is the backdrop for conflict over ideas. A university is archaic, dynamic, creative, and progressive all at once. The resultant productivity is enormous. It is when the conflict over ideas extends into conflict over the personalities and performance of people that the trouble starts.

CONFLICT ABOUT PEOPLE AND THEIR PERFORMANCE

Conflict, even serious and protracted conflict about people, can be productive. This realization has to do with the idea that priorities must sometimes be established that work against the few, for the best interest of the institution and the people who support it with tax dollars, tuition, and grants and contracts. This is consistent with the principle of basic fairness. Every instance of denial of tenure or promotion involves conflict, but lowering standards to avoid it is unfair to colleagues, the institution as a whole, taxpayers and tuition payers, not to mention students. The following examples provide insight into the productive side of conflict through two real situations.

> *In March 2003, the Nebraska governor proposed a 10% reduction in the operating budget of the University of Nebraska–Lincoln (UNL), amounting to $21 million. This was in addition to substantial previous cuts and would have left the university with no option but to cut programs to preserve the core strengths of the institution to the greatest extent possible.*
>
> *According to a March 10, 2003, UNL press release, Chancellor Harvey Perlman announced the first $7.5 million in proposed cuts in an electronic communication to the university community. His stated strategy was "to preserve the central strengths*

of the university and to position us to continue to enhance our programs of teaching, research, and service."

Initial proposals for programmatic reductions and discontinuances included elimination of the research division of the University of Nebraska State Museum. This would have resulted in the layoff of a number of tenured faculty members. Because tenure was involved, this proved to be one of the most hard-fought issues in the process. An Academic Planning Committee appointed to review the chancellor's proposals opposed this reduction.

By definition, Perlman's proposals amounted to a declaration of financial exigency, since tenured faculty would be laid off due to financial reasons. This is as intense an issue as can be raised in a university environment. In April 2003, the faculty senate at UNL mounted a vote of no confidence in Perlman. The chancellor, however, stated his intent to hold a university-wide faculty referendum on his proposals with the commitment that if it went against him, he would resign his position. The referendum was held in May and Perlman won by an overwhelming vote of 90%.

As stated in a June 6, 2003, press release from UNL, the Nebraska legislature substantively attenuated the governor's proposal, and the university's actual budget reduction was diminished.

This was a high-stakes situation where fairness to those losing their jobs had to be considered, along with the best interests of the rest of the faculty, the students, the taxpayers, the tuition payers, and those funding grants and contracts. The long-term viability of the institution was at issue. In addressing this matter head on, the chancellor involved the faculty, students, regents, legislators, and other constituents. Numerous hearings were held on campus and around the state. These sessions were summarized and advertised in a university press release on April 4, 2003. Perlman and his administration maintained focus on the long-term best interests of the institution. Although extremely controversial, everything he proposed was out in the open. In the face of intense conflict, he exhibited a characteristic of central importance in resolving disputes involving people and their performance: *courage.*

There is no contradiction between sticking to one's guns on issues of central importance and showing respect for the disputants and compassion for the affected parties. Fairness is not confined to those losing their jobs, although the maximum compassion and accommodation possible is due them. It also extends to all the stakeholders in the institution and across the state, present and future.

The UNL case is a classic example of constructive conflict involving people (and money). A large and pressing problem existed, and it had to be solved within a very compressed timeframe. Every potential solution involved conflict.

> *During the 1990s, legislators and boards of regents and curators became convinced that doctoral universities had gone overboard in research, resulting in the neglect of teaching and learning. This view was compounded by criticism on many fronts, including the popular press, of faculty productivity. Critics cited too much time spent on personal consulting and self-serving career advancement activities. The outcome was a general atmosphere of doubt as to the accountability of academe, especially public universities. Higher education was no longer seen to be a self-evident good. The logical object of these concerns was tenure, and the era of post-tenure review came into being, accelerated by the mechanism of legislation by fax. That is to say that when one governor, or one legislator, or one board of regents or trustees gets on to something, the rest soon follow because they all go to the same meetings and read the same literature.*
>
> *In spring 1995, the chair of the Kansas Board of Regents made an informal stop at the ongoing meeting of the Council of Chief Academic Officers (COCAO), representing the six Kansas regents universities. The board was about to issue a list of marching orders to the universities as a result of a long series of activities regarding faculty evaluation. The chairman's message to COCAO was clear and concise.*

"The board," I recall him saying, "is convinced the universities are very rigorous in hiring new faculty. We believe a great deal of progress is being made in annual evaluation. It is clear that the decision to grant tenure is taken very seriously and the standards used are high. However, there is not a shred of evidence that any of the universities have any handle at all on dealing with tenured faculty who cease to be productive. So, either the institutions are going to take care of this or the board will do it for them."

The ensuing discussion clarified that the issue was not incompetence, but rather low or no productivity. The point was made that a small number of competent faculty don't do much in spite of their ability. The issue really was chronic low achievement, and that is the name by which the board's policy became known. It also is the name by which the remedy is known in the university handbook at Kansas State University today. At Kansas State, the faculty senate president, many faculty leaders, and the provost were in agreement on several points: 1) there were very few faculty to whom the new board policy actually applied; 2) this issue would progressively erode the integrity of tenure in the eyes of regents, legislators, and the general public if not addressed; and 3) if done properly the policy could have a constructive effect, especially when linked with the existing policy of individualizing the distribution of faculty effort. The president of the faculty senate appointed a task force comprised primarily of faculty to begin work on drafting policy. He rightly believed the best approach was for the faculty to seize the initiative in developing the framework for the eventual policy. By this time, only three months were left in his year as president. This process continued, with some revision of the process through the presidency of his successor, and was approved after approximately 18 months of work and negotiation with the provost, during the term of yet a third president of the faculty senate. Opposition was fierce in some quarters, mainly because the new policy was seen as an attack on tenure. Those supporting it had the opposite view, that it would save tenure. When the dust settled, the faculty senate approved the policy by a two to one margin, and the provost signed it. The Kansas State policy became a modified version of triggered post-tenure review. During the process, however, one point of major conflict emerged between the provost and the faculty senate over the definition of the word overall.

The emerging new "chronic low achiever" policy was based on a thorough annual evaluation, which the university already had in place. When overall *performance fell below minimal standards (to be defined by each academic department, subject to approval by the dean and provost) for two successive years or any three out of any five years, the dean could move to dismiss a tenured faculty member for cause, if the individual did not respond to a required remediation plan.*

The assumption of most faculty members was that overall *allowed for an individual faculty member to not do much, or perform poorly, in one major area (research, for example) if performance in another major area was good enough to offset it. The provost took a very different view, which was that if performance in a major area of work fell below minimal standards, it would be unusual for that individual to meet minimal acceptable standards* overall. *The underlying premise was that if an individual had 30% or 40% of her effort allocated to (for example) research, but did none, the resources devoted to that part of the individual's time were wasted. This was unfair to other faculty, the institution at large, and taxpayers and tuition payers. Some faculty worried that this might open the door for a future vindictive department head or dean to assign a faculty member work that he knew was outside an individual's ability to perform in order to maneuver him into "failure to meet minimal standards" on the annual evaluation.*

The conflict over this issue was very significant. Even many who supported the policy in general terms opposed the provost's position.

However, the conflict also was very productive. In the last analysis, the original policy statement was appended with three additional paragraphs that allowed this issue to be addressed in the departmental documents governing annual evaluation, promotion and tenure, and minimal standards of performance.

Since the policy was created and implementing documents developed and approved in each of the academic departments (1997), between 20 and 30 tenured faculty have been designated as failing to meet minimal standards of performance. Some have responded to development plans and/or rearrangement of assignment in concert with the department head. A few have resigned, some have retired, and one has been dismissed for cause. A number of floundering careers have been redirected and salvaged as a result of this policy, partly because it is linked to increased emphasis on professional development and much greater emphasis on individualization of the allocation of faculty effort.

The linkage to individualization of faculty effort, or flexible pathways to success, is extremely important. The concept can be difficult to establish in academic institutions, especially those that emphasize research. However, it is one of the most important methods of leveraging resources and preventing unproductive conflict. It has been addressed both in a psychosocial context and in terms of scholarship (see Chapter 2).

The instance of dismissal for cause merits brief elaboration. As of this writing, it was the first and, as of 2004, only case of dismissal for cause in the United States resulting from post-tenure review in the 1990s, at least that was challenged in court. Followed closely by academics interested in these issues, including the American Association of University Professors and other organizations, and *The Chronicle of Higher Education,* the integrity of Kansas State University's new policy hinged on a successful outcome in the on-campus grievance and the litigation that succeeded it.

The underlying issues were whether the university was dealing fairly with the grievant and whether the new policy, if followed properly, would undermine the basic tenets of tenure. Fortunately, the grievant's academic department had well-conceived policies and procedures that conformed to those of the university, and they were followed. The administrative appeal procedures conformed to university policy. The grievance hearing panel, created according to policy by the president of the faculty senate, was comprised entirely of faculty and was unanimous in finding in favor of the university. The dismissal was subsequently upheld both in state district court and in state appeals court. If this case had been lost, the entire premise of the new policy would have been called into question. In all likelihood, this would have resulted in a great deal of new conflict regarding individual cases and the policy itself.

People debating and arguing about ideas sometimes get angry at one another. That is part of the process of conflict and can result from a healthy passion about one's work. Only when that anger continues and becomes fixated on another person, or when an administrator seems to retaliate against a party to the debate, or when an individual is marginalized or impugned, do personal issues begin to creep in and render the conflict unproductive.

2 ◆ A FRAMEWORK FOR UNDERSTANDING CONFLICT IN AN ACADEMIC ENVIRONMENT

INSTITUTIONAL CULTURE AND HISTORY

I grew up in Kansas and also lived and worked in Oklahoma and Missouri. These states are as different as day and night. Kansans are basically conservative and tend to keep their best features a secret; the Okies are wide open, high rolling, and colorful; and they don't call Missouri the Show Me State for nothing. So it is with institutions of higher education, be they small liberal arts colleges, community colleges, regional master's level institutions, or large research universities.

The applied nature of community colleges drives a different mission and culture than four-year institutions. The role and interests of the faculty and administration are customized accordingly. A community college in a large metropolitan area has a different ethos than one in a rural setting. For one thing, the latter has a much higher percent of full-time faculty. This also figures into the culture and governance issues in universities in large urban areas versus those in smaller communities. In small liberal arts colleges, students, faculty members, and administrators have much greater opportunity to know each other personally.

Each institution has traditions attached to annual events and specific places on campus that have grown over decades like moss on a rock. These local idiosyncrasies have great value because they contribute to a sense of place that tends to stay with students for a lifetime. Of course, this is more important for full-time students on a residential campus and matters not a whit for those who learn at a distance.

Different academic units have strikingly different cultural characteristics within a single institution. The culture of a mathematics department is markedly different from that of an agronomy department. Similarly, art and architecture may resonate on a similar frequency, but they differ wildly from mechanical engineering or chemistry.

These cultural variations across any institution, especially large ones, emphasize the importance of overarching guidelines and policies, as well as understood practices, that let the total organization function as a whole cloth. They also underscore the need for department-level documents that customize criteria and standards for annual evaluation, promotion and tenure, and some form of post-tenure review. Pounding square pegs into round holes creates chronic pressure and friction—an ideal seed bed for future conflict.

The resultant aggregation of policy and practice at the department, college or school, and institution-wide level is analogous to a perennial garden. The basic distribution of plants is well adapted to the location, but each plant needs pruning now and again, and weeds grow among them that require rooting out.

Institutional culture, practice, and procedure are also strongly affected by governance arrangements and the traditions encrusted around them. For example, the role of the faculty senate or assembly is very different if the institution has a contract with a bargaining unit. This is especially so with regard to the relationship between faculty governance and the administration.

Department heads and chairs play a very important role in dispute prevention and resolution. Nomenclature aside, if the person leading the department has both authority and responsibility beyond the basic paper-processing functions of the department as well as training in management and leadership, she can play a key role in this arena. However, if this individual is in a rotating role driven primarily by election for terms as short as three years, the head or chair's effectiveness is almost a matter of chance, and the role is very limited.

Whatever the cultural and historical characteristics of the institution, the policies and procedures, and the personality and style of those responsible for implementing them must be reflected in the system of dispute prevention, resolution, and management (DPRM) in each institution.

PERSONALITY AND EXPERIENCE OF THE RESPONSIBLE PARTIES

One of the most inane debates academic administrators can become embroiled in is the issue of substance versus style. The old argument is that what matters is for the dean to really know what she is doing and to make the right calls. If she gets the job done and makes good strategic decisions, her style should not be all that important. There is no point in arguing substance versus style. For anyone to succeed in academic administration today, he must have strong strategic skills and vision *and* a personality and style that is effective and matches the culture of the institution he serves. For the most part, administrators do not fail because they are dumb but because they either lack the ability to work with people or their personality and style do not fit the culture and collective personality of the institution.

An effective way to avoid unproductive conflict and further the institution is for a leader with vision to have good ideas and to recognize that the faculty and staff also have something to contribute. Involving faculty and staff in the decision-making process utilizes their imagination and experience, resulting in the best decisions possible as well as a feeling of ownership in the outcome, or at least a sense of being heard. Valuing faculty and staff input is not based on a person's prior academic success so much as on his ability to think strategically and engage people—most especially the people who make up the culture of the institution. A culture that values productive disagreement is one of the most effective means available to prevent unproductive disputes.

TRUSTWORTHINESS AND ACCEPTANCE

People on the receiving end of decision and action assume things happen for a reason. Allred (2000) addresses this concept within the framework of motive and attribution. If they think the reason for a decision was logical, even though they disagree with it, and a well-intended person took the action, they are less likely to take offense. This can have special importance in preventing and resolving disputes. Administrators make and implement many decisions everyday. It is hoped that the majority of these are good ideas, implemented well. However, some will prove to be bad ideas and some, good ideas implemented poorly. Whatever the case, those affected will attribute a motive to those making the decisions. This is so whether two individuals are involved, or large groups, for example, the faculty senate and the administration. If those affected trust (and like) the instigators, they are more likely to attribute positive motives for a given action. Similarly, if the internal logic of a decision or action holds up under scrutiny and is articulated clearly, positive motives are more likely to be attributed. Acknowledgment of mistakes (accompanied by a sincere apology) can be critical to differentiating common error from intentional action. The following example portrays a good decision implemented badly.

> *By any measure, High Plains University ran on a penurious budget and always had. It was mid-May, and the legislature had been floundering toward adjournment a month later than normal. Tom Franks, the provost, and Ned Wilson, the chief financial officer, were at the monthly meeting of the board of regents. The legislature had finally adjourned at 2:00 a.m., and it was evident early on that they had cobbled together an array of one-time fixes to get out of the session. No one had yet figured out what the effect would be on the institution's budget for the next fiscal year, which would begin in less than six weeks. The nine-month faculty was disappearing for the summer, and at least two of the seven deans were leaving within the week for some much needed vacation.*

About ten that morning, Wilson pulled Franks aside. "Moderling just called," he said. Mel Moderling was the budget director. He had been furiously analyzing the legislative mare's nest since 6:00 a.m. "He says the way the legislature made the numbers work was to make us self-fund the benefit pool and servicing new buildings. Since we are opening Fleming Hall in October, the two together leave us about $900,000 short."

That was enough to matter a lot, with a $250 million base budget and virtually no reserves. The president was in Washington DC, attending a board of directors meeting of a national organization, and Franks was representing him at the board meeting.

"Well," he replied, "time is really short. We had better get a meeting with the deans soon, like tomorrow. This is not going to be pretty."

The deans could not meet until early the following week. One dean had postponed his vacation. Another had a pile of money tied up in nonrefundable airline tickets and had left for the Maine coast. She was attending by way of a telephone hook-up situated in the middle of the conference table. By then the budget office had briefed the budget people in the colleges and the deans had the gist of the problem, but they needed guidelines from the administration and they always liked to compare notes. Some also wanted to lobby for the administration to use the rest of its reserves to cover the shortfall while others wanted differential cuts, with the graduate school and facilities taking the biggest hit.

Because it was so close to the start of the fiscal year and the central reserve already was depleted from a rescission the previous year, the cuts were prorated. It was less than .5% and shouldn't have been a huge deal, even late in the year. However, previous cuts during recent years had drained operating accounts to the point that some departments were hard pressed to buy basic necessities. A priority had been placed for years on maintaining positions at a level that ensured adequate class sections to preserve

*enrollments. When the deans sprung the new cuts on the depart-
ment heads, some went on the warpath, especially those that did
not have a research-based budget component that produced indirect cost recovery dollars or other flexible sources to draw on.
The have-nots in arts and sciences were hit hardest. The head of
the history department wrote an email to the dean of arts and
sciences and copied it to his faculty and to all the other heads in
the college. Within an hour, it had been forwarded just about
everywhere, including to the president of the faculty senate. Unfortunately, this was the first she had heard of the whole issue.
She was caught flatfooted. Worse still, the elections had just taken
place and a new president was taking over.*

The history head's email put everyone in a bind.

*"It is not the fault of the administration that the legislature
continued its practice of screwing the universities at the 11th
hour. However, it is irresponsible for the provost to fail to recognize that a last-minute cut like this, when we have contracts
with graduate teaching assistants and temporary faculty that we
can't break, will gut our operating account to the point that we
cannot cover basic costs. We already have some faculty paying for
copying handouts out of their own pockets. It seems self-evident
that the administration is not using reserves to cushion this because they want to continue expanding research in the sciences,
which is something the university cannot afford. Worse yet, it is
my understanding that the faculty leadership never was apprised
of this whole mess, let alone consulted. I assume no explanation
was provided to them because there is no reasonable basis for the
way this is being handled. At best, it is disrespectful, at worst
underhanded."*

*Faculty members remained upset about the episode through-
out the summer. When the university's moving parts began to
mesh in the fall, it heated up again. The provost was on the
front burner because he had announced the cuts and made the
decision to prorate them. He clearly made a bad mistake by not
contacting the faculty leadership and having a session similar to*

the one he held with the deans. That it was an oversight was of no immediate significance. As a result, his rationale was lost in the tumult, and he was portrayed as condescending and lacking appreciation for the humanities and fine arts. Not without reason. Each faculty senate president, both outgoing and incoming, was in no position to defend him. In fact, each was offended and embarrassed because they had been left out of the loop.

At the first opportunity, the provost met with the new faculty senate president and other officers in mid-August. In addition to explaining the background and logic of how the cuts was made, Provost Franks did the only legitimate thing he could. He apologized.

The whole episode began to get on a more positive trajectory in the first faculty senate meeting later that month. After 20 minutes of a dozen different faculty lambasting the administration generally, and Franks in particular, Esther Swenson, the new president-elect said, "I agree with much of what you all say, but we should give the provost credit for acknowledging that he screwed this up. And, he actually apologized. I can't remember an administrator apologizing for anything in the 20 years I have been here."

Obviously, Franks had no choice but to convene the deans and make the cuts. Reasonable people could disagree about how they were distributed. That he simply forgot to review his decision with the faculty leadership and solicit their input was a mistake, the kind of thing that breeds ill will unnecessarily. Acknowledging his mistake and apologizing differentiated a thoughtless oversight from something vindictive or devious. Given the underlying tension over the ever-shrinking budget, it could have been the issue that let things get out of hand. Franks recovered from a bad situation by recognizing that the error was his own and by apologizing to the right people. As a result, an unnecessary dispute that would have consumed time and money was avoided.

EMOTION: HEATING UP AND COOLING

Emotion is much like conflict in the larger sense. It can be an essential ingredient of making (good) things happen. Without emotion, our days would be pretty nondescript. But emotion can become destructive. One particular emotion is the most destructive of all: anger.

Things said in anger cannot always be withdrawn. Things written in anger certainly cannot. In days gone by, it usually took long enough for an angry person to write a letter and deliver it for the individual to cool down and reconsider, or at least to proofread it. Email changed all that. It is all too easy to type off a stream of consciousness in anger and hit "send," dispatching the venom into the ether, forever irretrievable. Once in writing, angry statements take on a life of their own and are extremely difficult to undo.

Some people rely on anger as a crutch in making decisions, especially hard ones involving people. One might survive as a faculty member doing this, but not in administration. For example, criticism of a subordinate's work, when needed, is very important for employer and employee alike. It should be done at the appropriate time, either at the moment of an incident, or in an annual evaluation, or at a time set aside for such an exchange. It should never be done in anger. No successful horse trainer would make a practice of disciplining a horse in training in anger (many unsuccessful ones do it routinely). We should expect the same minimal standard from a person with administrative responsibility in an academic institution. But some people cannot take action in opposition to someone else until they are angry, and that is exactly the wrong time.

Whether training horses or interacting with people in emotionally charged conflict, action and reaction can either escalate or deescalate a bad situation. If, for example, a brand new tenure-track assistant professor in the first month of teaching rushes into his department chairman's office angry and upset because a student's father just tried to intimidate him into raising his son's grade, and the chair stands in the door of his office listening with his arms folded across his chest, the situation might escalate; especially if he is holding his breath and getting red in the face because he sees a situation developing that he does not want to deal with. On the other hand, if he invites the young man to come in and have a seat, offers him something to drink, sits down across a coffee table from him (not across his desk) and, in a relaxed posture asks him to walk through the incident from the top, the situation can be converted into a logical problem-solving process.

A moment of high emotion can be a good time to identify a problem, but it is the wrong time to attempt to solve it. Fighter pilots and heart surgeons might have to act on split-second decisions made in the heat of the moment. For the most part, academic administrators do not. On the other side of the same coin is the need to address conflict, especially emotionally charged conflict, in a timely way. The need for both cooling down and timely action can be addressed in one two-part step: call time out and begin fact-finding and perspective-setting.

Returning to the assistant professor's situation, the chair has choices. He might say, "Jack, you are upset. Let's give this a little time and talk about it again when you calm down." This would suggest that the chair thinks the young man is just overwrought about nothing much and would escalate the problem emotionally. It also would let the fact-finding trail grow cold. A more productive course would be for the chair to:

- Be clear that this kind of intimidation attempt is not tolerated.

- Get the name of the student and the father's contact information.

- Arrange to meet again, before which the chair will have talked with the student and parent.

- Recognize the instructor's authority in how this actually is handled in terms of assessing student performance.

- Suggest that in all likelihood the two of them will meet together with the student and possibly the father as well.

In effect, this calls time out, while being clear that fact-finding will be immediate. It also makes clear that the chair will follow through, but not independent of the faculty member and his prerogatives as the instructor. It makes no commitment, *a priori*, as to assignment of guilt or blame.

FACT-FINDING, FRAMING, AND REFRAMING

Fundamentally, resolving a dispute is based on understanding what the dispute is really about. What the dispute is about and what actually happened in a given instance are different but related. However, what happened in a given incident is critical to resolving a dispute even though the roots of conflict may extend into deeper soil. "What happened?" is a matter subject to the establishment of facts, thus fact-finding must be thorough and timely. The framing and reframing process is part of the standard drill in interest-based negotiation and mediation, to be discussed later. It is the use of perspective-setting in moving the parties from their initial positions to the interests they really need to address. Here it is placed in a different context to demonstrate that it really plays a role in heading off any number of disputes when they first begin to sprout.

Fact-finding can only go forward after the problem to be solved is understood. This understanding must be the same for interveners and disputants alike. Framing the problem is a key first step. It must be kept in mind that one of the critical facts to be discovered is the underlying need of the parties to the dispute.

"Well," the dean might say, "having heard the conversation so far, here is my understanding of what happened and what the main issues are." This would then be followed by a concise summary.

This would likely be followed by a discussion, perhaps vehement, about the various misconceptions the dean has, along with possible attacks on the ability of a mathematician like the dean to see the point of view of someone from the art department. Such an incident might happen when the primary disputant's chief complaint is about the dean's uneven distribution of funds between the poverty-stricken art department and the grant and contract-rich geology department. The benefit is that additional facts would come to light and the various points of view would become clearer.

The dean might summarize again his understanding of the problem. He would reframe the situation based on the facts as he has come to know them at that point, including an understanding of the underlying needs or desires of the parties. Much can be accomplished in doing this. It helps the parties bring the situation into perspective. The relative importance of real and perceived needs can be established. This process begins to move the parties in the direction of taking part in creating a solution. As the activity goes forward, it may become clear that the issue at hand is not so important after all, except as a symbol of the reality that the head of the art department is sick and tired of that arrogant curmudgeon (according to her perception) that heads the geology department running over her every chance he gets. That would be progress indeed. Now the parties know what problem they really are trying to solve. The process can reach this point only through framing (the problem), fact-finding, interest identification, and reframing.

OWNERSHIP IN RESOLUTION

Engagement is the key to success in preventing or resolving disputes. Dancing around the issues heightens the tension, delays resolution, and increases collateral damage. Engagement leads to solving problems and preserving relationships. Only through engagement in framing, fact-finding, interest identification, and reframing, can the parties define problems and begin to take part in creating solutions.

Next to parking and possibly salaries, space may be the most hotly contested issue on campus. Whether the dean of engineering or the dean of business gets office and classroom space vacated in Ivy Hall as a result of the completion of Stone Hall can become a symbol of status and priorities. To give up space seems certain to diminish a dean or her college in the eyes of the faculty. Chief academic officers commonly encounter such situations. The first step in addressing them is to realize that deans are both smart and reasonable people. The provost will

engage the deans in a process of framing, fact-finding, interest identification, and reframing, individually and together. One of the best
means of engagement is to walk through the space at issue, as a group.
The walk works better if the campus space czar is along, armed with a
complete set of skeleton keys, in order to open every closed door and
observe all the space. The area currently occupied should be examined
thoroughly before the new space in Stone Hall is visited. The walk
should be long enough to tire everyone. As the parties get tired of looking at the space, they tend to become more interested in taking part in
solving the space problem.

Much fact-finding also happens on such a walk. A highly coveted
room may be revealed to be full of junk computers and file cabinets.
This may be news to the dean as well as the provost because she had
been listening to a department head's pitch on space without going and
examining it herself.

The walk offers many opportunities to start the parties thinking
about solutions. For example, the vice president might ask the space
czar, "Since business needs a bigger computer lab, how would it work
to take out this wall and make Ivy 210 and 211 into one big room?"
That is an idea that the two deans will have to respond to, regardless of
the space czar's answer. This will start a process that will lead to a resolution in which everyone is part owner. Even if the provost ultimately
resolves the issue by himself, the deans will understand the logic, they
will know their points of view were heard and understood, and they
will have furnished some of the ideas that went into the outcome. If the
right decision is made, neither one will be happy, but both are likely to
live with it and go on. Deans are usually pragmatic people.

RACE, GENDER, AND CONFLICT

There are two ways to address race, gender, and conflict: a lengthy discourse or a short summary of main points. The short version is in order
here, because the long one would make a monograph by itself.

There are two kinds of claims about discrimination and racial and
sexual harassment: those that state a legal violation and those that do

not. In those that do, the institution's obligation to act, in a relatively prescribed manner, is clear. If a claim or stated concern goes unaddressed, the case may be litigated in civil court, and the plaintiff has a good chance to prevail.

Some race and gender claims, if true, would meet the legal standard if substantiated. However, substantiation is not always feasible, even though the allegation is true. In those instances where it is not possible to prove either the guilt or innocence of the respondent, the classic he said–she said standoff could become the worst of all outcomes. The claimant never feels vindicated, and the respondent feels wrongly besmirched. The wounds continue to fester. Some of these cases are litigated. Relationships are damaged, often irreversibly, unless effective action is taken to resolve the residual conflict.

The most common situation arises from injurious actions, either real or perceived, that are racially or sexually motivated but when scrutinized by a qualified adjudicator would not, if true, meet the legal standard for discrimination or harassment. Whether official or unofficial, this finding can all too easily be construed as meaning no problem exists at all. In most instances, this is not the case. To drop the matter at that point is a serious mistake and an injustice to the claimant and the respondent. Their working relationship is likely to be permanently damaged and those around them are distracted by the ongoing conflict. It is imperative that parties to these matters be directed into another avenue of dispute resolution, to the extent they are willing. Often some persuasion and coaching is required to create an environment in which the parties are comfortable about pursuing resolution.

Rude, arrogant behavior is likely to be taken by most white men as just that. However, the lone woman or person of color in a large, busy department may very well personalize such behavior as related to race or gender. This is not unreasonable given an all too common history of marginalization or exclusion, unintended though it might have been.

The role and methodology of the Office of Affirmative Action or its equivalent is crucial here. White men are more likely to go up the chain of command (department head/chair, dean, provost), whereas women and faculty of color often go first to the Office of Affirmative Action, either because they have interpreted the offending behavior as race or gender related, or because they have been advised to do so by a friend or ombudsperson. If the matter is not demonstrated to be a result of the claimant's race or gender and is not pursued further, the underlying problem continues to fester, and the symptoms will spread.

The irony is that unless harassment is flagrant, the recipient just wants it to stop. The positive effects of stoppage will be enhanced by an apology. But this is not likely to happen if the only avenues available for mutual understanding and resolution are affirmative action complaint and grievance. The longer these issues persist, the harder the lines are drawn and the greater the lasting damage to working relationships and to the surrounding work environment.

BALANCING THE CENTRAL NECESSITY OF FAIRNESS WITH PROTECTING THE INSTITUTION FROM LITIGATION

Academic institutions tend to fear lawsuits. This can go beyond the common sense aspiration to make litigation a last resort in the interest of a cheaper, quicker resolution that might preserve working relationships and just be plain unadorned fear of being sued. This is so because if one is sued, others will assume that the lawsuit has basis: either a wrong was done or a mistake was made. This concern is exacerbated by the fact that if a dean or the provost is sued in a personnel action, the president and board of regents or trustees also are sued. The plaintiff might even throw in the governor for good measure.

Although it is true that litigation should be preserved as a last resort, fear of being sued is a poor starting place in dispute prevention and resolution and can cause a lot of unnecessary complications. Fear of losing a lawsuit is even greater than fear of being sued. Losing lawsuits is not good for the institution or the individuals in it, but attempts to avoid such a loss can negate the potential for early resolution of a dispute.

I come from a family of lawyers and have great respect for the elegant logic of the law and most of the people who practice it. Lawyers, including university lawyers, have done me much more good than harm. However, an understanding must be reached as to what values are being served in dispute resolution. It helps if the attorney(s) serving the institution really knows how an academic institution works, as well as the culture, tradition, and politics of the specific institution. Disputes are most readily resolved early in the conflict. To help facilitate a timely resolution and to preserve the institution's legal position for future contingencies, attorneys should be involved early in the conflict.

One of the most common pieces of advice lawyers give their clients is to say as little as possible, either verbally or in writing. Conversely, the key to preventing and resolving disputes is for the parties to say everything they can think of that might be pertinent to a resolution as early as possible. On balance, lawyers should not be present in such situations. In order to resolve disputes, complete candor is necessary. One can be candid and discrete at the same time, however, and a good attorney who really understands the institution can help this happen by way of an advisory role.

It should be noted that mediation, which will be discussed in Chapter 3, can play an important role in serious disputes. This is so for many reasons, one of which is that according to most Agreements to Mediate, what is said in the mediation is not admissible in court. Ideas can be floated and offers can be made that cannot be misrepresented later as commitments or agreements. The mediator cannot be subpoenaed in a court proceeding. Lawyers can be present or absent, depending on the agreement by the parties.

RIGID VERSUS FLEXIBLE CAREER PATHS

Academic institutions are divided according to disciplines. Within each of these departmentalized categories, there is a tendency to cast all faculty members into one mold, somewhat like peas in a pod. However, people are different and change over time. This has long been recognized, but systemic efforts to address it can be difficult to sustain. The burnout and subsequent bitterness and disengagement created by inflexible academic stereotyping are major causes of lost resources and unproductive conflict.

In 1978, Kanter summarized this in terms that can serve us just as well today:

> People who perceive an opportunity to grow (the movers) in their careers develop high aspirations and become highly work involved. In contrast people who see little opportunity to progress professionally (the stuck) tend to limit their aspirations, appear to become less motivated and begin gradually to disengage from their work. Movers characteristically are energetic and highly productive. The stuck are more likely to become passive gripers from the sidelines, what we in higher education often refer to as deadwood. (p. 2)

Boyer (1990) laid the groundwork for addressing this dilemma in terms of how the academy defines and values scholarship. The effective use of Boyer's concept of identifying scholarship in discovery, integration, application, and teaching begins by no longer using the terms *research* and *scholarship* interchangeably. This basic step creates a level of flexibility sufficient to address the concerns raised by Kanter. In the process, a very large body of conflict can be mitigated and the work of the institution enhanced.

3 ◆ Methods of Conflict Resolution in an Academic Environment

Informal Resolution: Counseling, Coaching, and Facilitation

A discourse on creating an integrated system of prevention, resolution, and management of conflicts and disputes can all too easily leave out or under-emphasize the importance of informal methods. Many issues are handled informally, and this is the best approach when it works. Informal counseling sometimes is best viewed as part of a system in order to be applied optimally. The following story of academic ethics, aspirations of tenure and promotion, and rampaging egos creates a realistic example.

> *Marcel Short, assistant professor of anthropology, published his dissertation within a year, picked up four Ph.D. students within two years, and pulled in a large foundation grant going into year three. Short was investigating the question of whether an underground Jewish community really emerged in the southwest United States as part of the Spanish conquest and subsequent immigration, or whether the signs of such were mere aberrations. For example, were menorahs turning up in small Hispanic villages as northern New Mexico family heirlooms carried over from Jews fleeing the Inquisition or merely artifacts acquired by early immigrants and brought to New Spain without religious*

significance? It was the kind of controversy that caught public attention, and somehow Short had quickly risen to the upper echelon of the relevant scholarship.

For the first year or so after his arrival in the Department of Anthropology at Middle State University, Short had collaborated off and on with Lincoln Atwood, a full professor whose work always had reflected a fascination with the evolution of religion in primitive cultures. Atwood had become a mentor of sorts for Short and, at times, they had shared interests. In recent years, Atwood had devoted much of his attention to the religious tendencies of the Anasazi and the question of whether a Kachina-based religious fervor had been a primary or secondary reason for their departure from the four corners to the northern Rio Grand region. While poking around Taos Pueblo, he had come across some references to the Spanish Jew question and passed them along to Short, as it related to some other work the assistant professor was doing on the Catholic mission system and exploitation of Indian populations in the region. In fact, Atwood had provided Marcel Short with a monograph (fresh off the copy machine from the University of New Mexico library) on the topic and a personal letter giving his views on the potential validity of the idea. Atwood also made passing reference to the subject in a popular article he wrote for the Denver Post, *the primary subject of which was the out-migration of the Anasazi, their role in the establishment of the Rio Grande pueblo system, and their eventual encounter with Catholicism.*

Atwood had been happy to see Short's career taking off. When his young colleague had received a small summer grant to spend a couple of months in northern New Mexico to study the question, Atwood had thought nothing of it. However, when Short published a preliminary paper on his findings, and Atwood's role was not mentioned, Atwood noticed it. As a result of his initial paper, which was insightful and very readable, Short was invited to present at several conferences. He continued to pursue the subject as one of his research interests.

A month ago, Short had published a lengthy review paper on Crypto Judaism in northern New Mexico in a major journal. Again, Atwood's contributions to his early work were not mentioned. One might have argued that, while this pushed the ethical margins, it did not cross them, except for one small point. Short's paper contained a direct quote from Atwood's letter to him at the time he received the monograph, but it included no attribution.

Atwood was furious, disappointed, and angry. Most of all, he was alarmed at what he saw to be a pattern of self-aggrandizement, topped by outright academic dishonesty. He stewed about it for a week and knew he could not let it go. Finally, he went to see the head of anthropology, Anna Morrison. So far, he had talked to no one else about the matter.

When Atwood had laid out the whole scenario to Morrison, he summed up with his main concern. "Anna," he said, running his hand through his curly gray hair, "you and I have been colleagues in this department for a long time. Let's set aside any bias I might have as a result of a bruised ego from Short not acknowledging my help in the first place. This piece of outright plagiarism is something we have never had before. I can't imagine we want someone in our department, no matter how brilliant he might be, who would do such a thing."

Morrison knew this was a good time to think before speaking. She liked and respected Atwood. He was a good scholar with high standards. He clearly believed Short's actions to be wanton plagiarism. As she looked at the review paper in one hand and Atwood's letter in the other, her old colleague did have a point. The matter could not be ignored. Plagiarism could not be condoned on any scale. On the other hand, to Anna this appeared not to be a major incident. Given that almost two years had passed between the time Atwood wrote his letter and Short wrote his paper, it might even be conceivable that it was an oversight, albeit a very unfortunate one. Either way, it could cost Short his job and eventual tenure and seriously damage his career. More specifically, he had a mid-probationary review coming up in a couple of months, and this would have to be addressed before or during that process.

"Do you mind if I make copies of these?" she asked. "I must confront Dr. Short about this matter, and I want to have the evidence in front of us when I do."

Atwood thought for a moment, but then agreed. He hesitated because he felt perhaps he should go directly to Short himself. But he also realized this was a department matter, which is why he spoke to Morrison first.

Morrison decided that they would meet with Short together, and that is what happened, two days later.

Morrison had them seated around a round table in the corner of her office. She unfolded the copy of the relevant page from Short's paper and slid Atwood's letter alongside it. "Dr. Short," she said in an even tone, watching his face intently, "we need an explanation of this." With each index finger, she pointed at the highlighted phrase, identical in each paper.

Short looked at one paper, then at the other. Then he looked up at Atwood, then at Anna Morrison. His lower lip began to tremble. He looked down again, and slumped back in this chair. "Oh, dear God," he muttered.

Silence prevailed for a long moment. Finally Short gathered himself together. Sitting upright, he said, "This is devastating at best, but I would like to explain how I think it happened."

Atwood could not restrain himself. "How could you not know how it happened?" he almost yelled.

Short looked at Anna, who nodded that he should go ahead. As she did so, she placed a hand on Atwood's arm.

"Looking back," Short began, "I have been on an ego trip on the whole Crypto Judaism thing. I know Lincoln gave me the idea and the monograph that got my interest going. I even remember he wrote a letter to go with it. I should have mentioned his contribution any number of times. The truth is, I let my ego run away with me."

Morrison looked him in the eye. "That might just make it into the young and foolish category," she said, "but what about the quote?"

Short looked directly at her. He knew full well his career was at risk, at least this part of it. "The truth is," he said, "I incorporated that line into my thinking about the subject a long time back. When I wrote this paper several months ago, I thought it was a great phrase and used it without ever thinking of it as anyone else's. It just came out as part and parcel of my own thought process."

And there it was. Either you believed him or you didn't. Atwood didn't, at least at first. Morrison thought it might feasibly have happened as Short described. In any event, they had to decide what to do about it. Morrison ended the meeting and set up another one two days later. At that time, she laid out a take it or leave it approach that was agreed upon by both Short and Atwood.

Short wrote a letter to the tenured faculty in the anthropology department. Anna Morrison handed out copies at a specially called meeting. When they were read, she gathered them up and the departmental shredder consumed them immediately after the meeting. Except for one. That one she kept in her personal files until after Short's upcoming mid-probationary review. In the letter, Short apologized for his thoughtless disregard for Atwood's help. He acknowledged that he had quoted from his colleague's letter without attribution. He expressed regret for this lapse and apologized for his negligence, while still asserting very clearly how it came about.

When Short's mid-probationary review took place two months later, he was retained. However, a split vote by the faculty followed two hours of impassioned debate. The day came, two years later, when he was tenured and promoted. In the mid-probationary review, Lincoln Atwood argued for his continued appointment, having reached the conclusion in the intervening months that Short had made an honest mistake and owned up to it.

Anna Morrison's level head and common-sense approach maintained the academic integrity of her department and probably saved Short's career. She very easily could have gone off in all directions, leaving her department in confusion and ongoing conflict and ending Short's academic career as a side effect of controversy.

NEGOTIATION

A plethora of literature exists on the subject of negotiation. The purpose of this discussion, however, is not to conduct a literature review but to place negotiation in the toolbox of the prevention, resolution, and management of disputes in academe. Negotiation is a process of give and take based on the interests of the parties to the dispute. The trick is to determine what those interests are. They are frequently straightforward and involve such issues as the distribution of space in a new building or allocation of new tuition receipts or budget reductions. However, as noted in the section on fact-finding, framing, and reframing in Chapter 2, the interests actually may involve underlying concerns that only are symbolized by a specific disputed incident or situation.

Negotiation is an informal process aimed at getting the parties in a dispute to play creative roles in arriving at a solution that they can live with. It might be led by one of the parties or conducted formally or informally by a third party. It might take place in the student union over lunch or in an office or conference room. Negotiation might all happen in one sitting, or, much more likely, over several short sessions. In academic settings, ombudspersons can play an important role in the process as shuttle diplomats, witnesses, or both.

A tenured associate professor with a long history of disruptive behavior and limited productivity is the subject of repeated complaints by students and, more recently, parents. A growing number of individuals have accused the professor of temper tantrums and abusive behavior. Recently, he was alleged to have screamed at a student and shoved him for breaking an unusual glass bottle unearthed at an early 19th century trading post site on an archeology field trip. The student had fallen into a nearby ditch and broken his elbow. The professor admits "speaking sharply" to the student, but denies pushing him. Other students on the trip relate that they were not subjected to physical contact, but indicated the instructor had lost his temper with more than one of them. While no one saw the alleged shoving incident, they all agree that the injured student told them about it immediately afterward, and they believed him. Two of them had taken him to a nearby hospital for treatment. A week later, a recent graduate calls the head of the department. He relates that he has heard about this incident and remembers that a similar thing happened to him. In his case, the professor had grabbed him by his shirtfront and screamed in his face. He did not report it then, but now wishes he had. The alum says he had a good grade going and just wanted to take it and run.

The department head reaches the conclusion that the professor should be dismissed. He is compelled by the ongoing combination of disruptive behavior, evidence that students are being abused, and negligible productivity on the part of the professor. On a previous occasion the head already knew about, in which the professor threw a wet sponge at a graduate student, he had agreed to seek anger management treatment but had not followed through.

The recommendation for dismissal is made to the dean, who agrees with the decision after interviewing the professor (who still denies the allegations), the student making the complaint, and the alumnus. The recommendation is forwarded to the provost for action.

Upon interviewing the professor, the dean, the department head, the injured student (accompanied by his parents), the alumnus, and other students and faculty, the provost is confronted with a dilemma. As a result of these interviews, he learned of two other recent graduates who may have been subjected to

35

some kind of physical contact by the professor. He believes, as did the department head and dean, that in addition to his generally disruptive behavior, this person really does have a history of abusive treatment of students. There is good reason to believe that the man's behavior may have crossed the line to battery on at least two occasions. The police are looking into a possible battery charge in the current case, but the absence of third party witnesses makes it unlikely. The provost found the injured student's testimony very compelling. The difficulty is that he also believes there is a real risk of losing in a university-level grievance. His reasons for this concern include the fact that the professor's tenure is at stake. That could have a strong influence on a grievance panel, depending on its constituency. He also knows that the selection of a grievance panel is largely a random process. The provost also is concerned that some of the witnesses will be hard to assemble (especially the alumnus, who lives 2,000 miles away), and that the professor is sure to have some vociferous support from colleagues who see him as being railroaded. In fact, three such individuals already came to see him on the professor's behalf during his inquiry.

The provost believes that if the matter eventually goes to court, the parties are almost certain to be ordered to attempt mediation. Some judges will push the mediation issue to the point of a near mandate to settle. This always involves giving something up, usually money. He also suspects that the chances of winning in court are limited, primarily by the possibility of losing a grievance. At this point the provost makes two lists as follows.

A speculative assessment of the interests of the professor:

1) He is within two or three years of being able to draw social security and probably will need to be able to bridge that gap with some supplemental income.

2) He is six or seven years away from eligibility for Medicare and maintaining health care insurance is likely to

be a big issue. However, he is eligible for retirement and is assured of participation in the university health care plan but would have to pay the entire premium himself. This would occur, however, only if he retires as distinct from being fired.

3) He owns a number of rental houses, according to common wisdom, and these may provide a basic income stream. As an aside, the provost recalls more than one incident in which elected officials complained about the professor mowing the lawn of his rental properties during the workday.

4) He seems to be a basically unhappy person and is bitter about his experience at the university. Perhaps he would like to leave under the right circumstances.

Interests of the university:
1) The university would be better off replacing the professor, given his low level of productivity, long history of disruptive behavior, and apparent uncontrollable temper and abuse of students. While the physical aspect of student abuse has not been proven, the evidence is strong enough to be very concerned about it.

2) A standard process of dismissal, grievance, and lawsuit would be very costly in terms of widespread disruption among faculty, staff, and students, commitment of time by innumerable people, and out of pocket cost to the institution.

3) The possibility of the university losing a campus grievance and possibly in court is significant; an opinion shared by the university attorney.

4) There is the possibility that the professor actually is innocent of the worst of the allegations, although this would

require some sort of conspiracy between the current stu-dent and the recent graduate, who seemed not to have known each other when the alleged incidents occurred. Exploration of a separation agreement would indicate to the professor that the chances of dismissal for cause were high (this could be stated explicitly) and would give him an opportunity to choose if he wanted to fight the allega-tions or leave.

After assessing the two lists, the provost decides to explore the possibility of a settlement agreement. The university attorney agrees this approach has merit. The provost then meets with the professor and an ombudsman. The ombudsman, a historian of long and good standing, has worked with the professor earlier in the matter to advise him of his rights and to clarify procedures such as appeal, grievance, and affirmative action reviews. The provost tells the professor directly that, as he knows, dismissal has been recommended for reasons with which he is familiar. He further indicates that he is leaning toward supporting that recommendation. Before proceeding in that direction, however, he states his desire to learn whether the professor would be inter-ested in exploring some kind of negotiated agreement that would include his resignation. The ombudsperson is witness to the fact that the man was not pressured and that no specific offer or com-mitment was made.

The professor agrees to think it over. Within two days, the provost receives word through the ombudsman that the professor would like to receive a proposal. A process is initiated in which each party reviews options with his attorney, but lawyers are not involved directly in the exchange. The ombudsperson becomes a shuttle diplomat between the professor and the provost. The pro-vost's assessment of the professor's interests was pretty close to the mark. The outcome is that the professor agrees to retire without being designated as emeritus but with all other privileges of re-tirement, including continuing eligibility for medical insurance at his own expense. In return, he is to receive a cash payment that will significantly help meet the cost of medical insurance. The agreement includes a confidentiality clause. It does not become a matter of campus conversation and speculation and never appears in the press.

Reasonable people could argue long and hard about whether this fictionalized case was handled appropriately or not. However, it is used as an example of interest-based negotiation for two reasons. It does exemplify the process of moving from strongly held positions to the interests the parties need to address. It also exemplifies a form of raw pragmatism that sometimes is essential in the resolution of a dispute and negation of its potential for collateral damage, including an ongoing furor that drains the intellectual energy of a large number of people for a long period of time.

MEDIATION (INTEREST-BASED)

While it borders on splitting hairs, the discussion of mediation will be divided into interest-based and advisory, or rights-based, modalities. The difference between the two marks the point where the dispute resolution process moves from procedures based on the underlying needs and interests of the parties to those based on their rights.

Interest-based mediation may be defined as a voluntary process of facilitated negotiation in which a neutral third party, a professional mediator, sits down with the parties in conflict and helps them look for mutually acceptable solutions to work-related issues in dispute. The mediator does not make the decisions but works with the parties to identify their needs and interests and to develop creative options for resolving the conflict in a confidential manner.

One can see immediately how this process differs from negotiation as portrayed in the previous section. In the example used, there was no neutral third party involved other than the ombudsperson acting as a go-between. There was no assurance that the negotiation process would remain confidential. Either party could have quoted various aspects of it out of context. Any aspect of it would be subject to discovery in a lawsuit. All of the parties, including the ombudsman, would be subject to subpoena. None of the parties had agreed to any particular process or ground rules to define it, so it was subject to coming unhinged at any point. Interest-based mediation solves many of these problems, yet it is entirely voluntary.

In interest-based mediation, such as one would expect to utilize in an academic institution, the process is agreed to by the parties in the form of an Agreement to Mediate that is an approved part of institutional policy. This defines the ground rules for the process in advance. The complicating factor is that both (all) parties to the dispute must agree to mediation, and that can be difficult to achieve.

One of the most important advantages of mediation to all the parties to a dispute is the level of confidentiality to which the disputants are bound by the Agreement to Mediate. This prohibits the parties from repeating the content of the proceedings outside of the meetings. Agreements made in mediation are not legally binding, although one element of a resolution might be to create a separate legally binding agreement. Statements made during a mediation process cannot be used against a party in subsequent legal proceedings. The mediator is not subject to subpoena except in certain instances where criminal activity or intent is evident.

The mediator should be drawn from a list of university-approved, certified (by the state judiciary) mediators, none of whom should be university employees. This ensures the parties that they will not rub shoulders with the individual in the future and that the matter in dispute will not become part of the campus rumor mill, even inadvertently, by way of the mediator. It also relieves the institution of the problem of having one or more full-time mediators who will gradually accrue baggage, eventually need to be replaced, and be difficult to dismiss.

ADVISORY MEDIATION (RIGHTS-BASED)

Rights-based (advisory) mediation differentiates a form of mediation that is often less than completely voluntary, in that it usually takes place as a step in the process of litigation. This differentiation marks a major step in the spectrum of dispute resolution. In most instances of personnel law, the court will suggest, even demand, that the parties attempt to mediate. On occasion, depending on the disposition of the legal counsel involved, the disputants may elect to undertake mediation on their own. In either instance, the resultant mediation is, by definition, part of litigation. A sitting judge (on a volunteer basis), a practicing attorney agreed upon by the parties, or a retired judge will ordinarily be the mediator. Attorneys representing the parties are involved directly in the mediation. The interests of the parties still play a central role in the process, but it is very much directed by the relevant law and the strengths and weaknesses of each disputant's case from a legal perspective.

In a typical mediation of this type, the mediator will meet with the parties and their attorneys and review his understanding of the issues and how they relate to the lawsuit. He then will ask each party to clarify any discrepancies. Following this clarification and framing phase, the mediator is likely to place the parties in different rooms and meet with them privately. His goal in this phase is to point out to each party the weaknesses of their case and the strength of the opponent's. Each litigant's attorney will be directly involved in this process, advising their clients as to their rights and best negotiating position. The mediator also will push each party to put a proposal on the table, then shuttle back and forth with the intention of reaching a compromise settlement. The goal is to produce a legally binding agreement, in principle, that will be refined, completed, signed, and notarized in as short a time as possible.

Beyond the willingness of the parties to compromise, the success of this form of mediation, which can be very valuable and effective, leans heavily on the effectiveness of the mediator. The good ones are assertive and have outstanding skills at framing and reframing within the legal context of the dispute. They are not shy about explaining to the disputants how easily they could lose in court and what the consequences would be. The poor ones simply move back and forth, asking if either party has any ideas as to settlement of the case. This seldom, if ever, is successful.

APPEAL

Every faculty handbook or equivalent contains, or should contain, policy about appeal and grievance procedures integral to the institution's approach to due process. In institutions that have a contract with a union or bargaining unit, this likely will be part of the contract with the union, rather than part of the handbook (which in most institutions has the force of a contract). In many instances, these are the only steps in the due process system. One should appreciate that an effective approach to the prevention, resolution, and management of unproductive conflict makes appeal and grievance procedures pieces of a much bigger whole. Recognizing that there are many variations on the theme, appeal is described here as an administrative process and grievance as the last on-campus review process, most commonly conducted by a panel of peers that results in recommendations to the president, chancellor, or possibly the governing board. Thus, the appeal process stops with the chief academic officer or appropriate vice president.

The appeal process proceeds from the beliefs and needs of one or more parties but is conducted as a rights-based undertaking. That is to say, once a dispute has reached the point of a formal appeal, the aggrieved party has come to the belief that her rights have been violated. An appeal is an administrative proceeding. In academic settings it is commonly made at successive administrative levels. For faculty and academic staff, this culminates in an appeal to the provost or her equivalent. The result is in the form of an administrative ruling, not an equivocal proposal.

The appeal process still offers a great deal of flexibility. As facts emerge, so do options, although in instances of tenure denial they are few indeed. The process itself can still lead to facilitation and mediation efforts and these can be directed as part of the administrative finding, assuming reasonable evidence exists that they might be successful. This is especially so in instances of disputes about salary adjustment, annual evaluation, or even promotion.

In institutions that grant tenure, the most common appeal of a serious nature is about denial of tenure and promotion. For the administration, regardless of the issue, the appeal finding represents a definitive step. If the finding is in favor of the appellant, angst about the specific incident under dispute ends or dissipates, although other aspects of a larger conflict from which it arose may persist. It should be kept in mind that if the finding is in favor of the appellant, there are going to be other individuals who will not be pleased, usually a dean or department chair or both, not to mention a cohort of departmental faculty in tenure denial cases. The internal logic of the finding must be sufficient to make clear to all parties that the outcome was the result of fact-finding and careful reasoning, not rolling over to avoid further conflict. If the finding is against the appellant, then the entire matter becomes one of winning or losing. It is not in the interest of the institution, its other employees, or others who depend upon it, to lose grievance hearings or lawsuits. The letter, written by the administrator to the appellant, must be respectful in tone, regardless of the message. However, the internal logic and attention to issues of fairness to all parties must be crafted from the beginning in a manner intended to withstand any level of future scrutiny and to be the basis of winning in a future grievance or lawsuit. If either individual administrators or the institution make a habit of losing in litigation, their ability to settle disputes by any means is seriously diminished. Some cases require a stick as well as a carrot.

GRIEVANCE

The grievance process, normally conducted by a panel of peers, is the last due process step internal to the institution. It comes in two basic forms—simple and complicated. There is something to be said for each.

The simplest approach to the grievance is for a panel of peers, within a framework of previously established policy and procedure, to hear a presentation of the facts from each of the disputing parties and make a finding. This takes on the form of arbitration, subject to the intervention of the president or board. Attorneys would not be involved in the proceedings, although they might be advising either or both of the parties. The disadvantage to this approach is that it is more subject to appearing (or actually being) tainted by arbitrary or capricious action.

When attorneys advise the panel and each of the disputants during the grievance process, the likelihood of post-hearing disagreement about the propriety of the procedure is lowered. However, the required detail of the guiding policy, as well as the length and laborious nature of the proceedings, is much increased. Hours can turn into days. Attorneys can be involved at two levels: as advisors who are present but do not participate directly, and as direct participants. The latter is most likely to be reserved for instances of dismissal of a tenured faculty member.

Even as nonparticipant advisors, attorneys have a major impact on the proceedings. They supply a steady stream of suggestions and questions to disputants, advocates, and respondents and take copious notes. In fact, the attorneys are preparing for the litigation phase in case there is one, which usually happens if the grievance goes against the interests of the grievant. In effect, the grievance process becomes a form of pretrial discovery.

The availability of an attorney to guide the hearing panel is especially valuable. The results of grievance procedures have a strong tendency to lead to litigation, especially if conducted improperly. For the most part, this means interpretation of, and compliance with, the institution's own policy for the conduct of a grievance. If the hearing was not conducted appropriately, the finding is more vulnerable to being reversed during litigation than would otherwise be the case.

INTERVENTION BY STATE AND FEDERAL AGENCIES

Agencies like state Human Rights Commissions and Equal Employment Offices occasionally become involved at some point in personnel issues. Institutional representatives can approach these proceedings from a standpoint of antagonism or view these agencies as people trying to do their appointed task as fairly as possible. The latter usually yields better results.

Conceptually, these entities tend to operate like a state-level affirmative action office. They assess a given complaint to determine if it is serious or frivolous. If the matter appears to be potentially serious, they will conduct an investigation after obtaining a response from the institution. An attorney normally makes this response because complaints to these agencies have a good chance of being an initial step in the development of a lawsuit. Thus, the allegations made by the complainant and the content of the response are important parts of the discovery process in the event of litigation. Almost by definition, these proceedings are adversarial.

They also offer one more opportunity to settle the dispute prior to going to court. This is so primarily because an arm's length third party has become involved and, through her own process of framing, fact-finding, interest identification, and reframing, can develop a new perspective that might engage the disputants in creating the beginning of a settlement. This is helpful when the individual is objective and effective, as most of them are. The case officer frequently will act as a facilitator in pursuing the development of such an agreement. In most instances, if unable to broker an agreement, he will undertake to move the parties toward mediation.

Those cases that are investigated conclude with a finding of probable cause or not probable cause and a proviso that notifies the complainant of the right to file a lawsuit.

LITIGATION

Litigation is a circumstance in which one or more of the parties to a dispute have filed a lawsuit. While there are several layers of litigation that can ensue, these all are part of one laborious and expensive process. In most instances, an officer of the court, usually the judge under whose jurisdiction the lawsuit will be tried, will order the parties to attempt mediation. They also can do this of their own volition at any time.

In colleges and universities, the large majority of litigated cases derive from disputes involving tenure denial, dismissal, or the aftermath of a sexual harassment or racial discrimination claim. Some are a combination of more than one of these. Litigation is no longer about preserving working relationships, at least not fundamentally. It is about winning and losing. Given a choice, an institution should never enter into litigation that it does not have solid reason to believe it can win. Losing in court hurts the institution's image, undermines its ability to resolve or manage future disputes, and encourages future litigants. Throughout litigation, it is in the institution's interest to reach a settlement, unless the odds of winning are very good.

In some instances, agents of the institution may feel a case should go to court on principle, even if it is lost. However, the longer the process grinds on, the more realistic the parties become, especially those who are personally paying lawyer fees. When the cost is measured in direct out-of-pocket costs and in terms of human factors, only the rare case is worth going all the way to the courtroom.

In an academic environment, the parties must keep in mind that all litigation takes place in a fishbowl. Not only do newspapers and other media tend to update the public on these proceedings once a lawsuit has been filed, but various interests within the institution also follow it, especially when the matter is attended by a perceived breach of basic fairness or when a principle about policy is at stake. The collective drain on the intellectual resources of the institution can become formidable and far exceed the out-of-pocket cost of defending litigation in federal district court. Better to have the faculty of the Department of Chemistry debating the physical characteristics of a nanoparticle than whether the university is going to lose its latest lawsuit.

4 ◆ Policy and Procedure: Development and Implementation

The Influence of the Institution's History and Value System

Policy pertinent to the operation of an institution's approach to conflict resolution will accrue, at least in part, over a long period of time. The aggregated result may well be a disparate collection of policy for affirmative action issues, appeal and grievance, promotion and tenure, and so forth that have been cobbled together over a generation or two. They may not make a logical whole. How the relevant body of policy and procedure is arranged and implemented will be influenced significantly by whether the institution has a union or bargaining unit and what role it has. The history of the institution also results in a value system that is, to a significant extent, unique.

A liberal arts college is more likely than a large urban university to have a predominance of full-time employees, and many will have known most of their colleagues for years. The students will develop a sense of place quickly. Policy and practice may be part of a tradition that is widely understood, for better or for worse.

The mission of a community college is strikingly different from that of a four-year institution of any kind, urban or rural. This requires a much different approach to policy and procedure. It also is the case that many community colleges develop a network of distributed locations. This creates issues of educating full- and part-time employees as to policy and how it affects them individually.

A land-grant university in a small town will differ greatly from a state institution in a large city. The most obvious reason is that most of the faculty in the former will be full-time employees and part of a tight-knit university community. An urban university will have a large number of part-time faculty and part-time students. As a result, the core community may be much smaller. This means that a collective understanding about a body of policy and procedure can be much more difficult to establish. At the same time it may be less critical because part-time employees are easier to replace.

Regardless of these differences, key issues are held in common. How they are addressed through policy and procedure must be appropriate for the individual institution. Multiple aspects must comprise a coherent body of policy. They must be clear and easy to access and understand. They are administered in a context of understood practices that also must be observed. In effect, this collection of policy, procedure, and practice becomes the canon law of the institution. Proactive strategies must be available to ensure that every individual understands how the place works and what course of action is available when problems arise. The canon law must make sense with the relevant civil law, and together the two comprise the total architecture of the institution's approach to dealing with unproductive conflict.

EDUCATING THE INSTITUTIONAL COMMUNITY: CLARITY OF POLICY AND PROCEDURE

The relevant categories of policy go well beyond those for appeal and grievance and should include annual evaluation, promotion and tenure, the local version of post-tenure review, appeal and grievance, sexual harassment, racial and gender discrimination, and any specific items related to these issues or to dispute resolution per se. For example, the institution may have separate policy on mediation and arbitration. As will be noted in Chapter 7, an institutional statement of core values is important. It is critical to recognize that these cannot be viewed as disparate activities. *They all are essential threads in creating a whole cloth of dispute prevention, resolution, and management (DPRM).* Each will be placed in context conceptually here as follows.

ANNUAL EVALUATION

Tomes have been written about faculty evaluation. Much of it makes for valuable reading. The purpose here, however, is not to address the nuances of annual evaluation, but to place it and its basic components in a context of the entire body of policy and procedure pertinent to DPRM. Annual evaluation of a faculty or staff member's performance has three basic objectives. The first is to assess performance over the year just ended. The second is to look forward to the coming year (or other appropriate period), establish goals, and allocate time and effort in ways that optimize the contribution of the individual's strengths to the collective achievement of the unit. Of course, this works in practice somewhat differently for tenure-track faculty than for those who are tenured. The third is to relate performance to the application of the reward system. Given that the time and talent of the faculty are the chief resource of the institution, this process is a resource allocation procedure as well as an aid to career development and program improvement in the process of implementing the reward system in response to annual productivity.

When the annual performance evaluation is treated as a means of distributing salary increases only, trouble is sure to follow. In lean years, it might not be done at all or in a slipshod manner. The annual evaluation does not take place in a vacuum. It is part of an overall resource utilization process aimed at keeping careers productive and successful and optimizing the deployment of faculty time and talent—the only thing the institution really has to sell.

Feedback in each annual evaluation has a role in the promotion and tenure process. When individuals are denied tenure or promotion based on reasons that are not consistent with the feedback provided by past annual evaluations (and the mid-probationary review), the denial is more likely to be seen as arbitrary and capricious, departing from written rules and regulations, or discriminatory. This is so because such inconsistency does not pass the basic fairness test.

PROMOTION AND TENURE

Tenure is the single most common cause of serious disputes in an academic environment wherein it is part of policy and practice. Clear and effective policies and procedures governing the granting of tenure are a critical aspect of dispute prevention. It is necessary to consider promotion and tenure together since both processes tend to happen in tandem during the same cycle in any given year. In most instances, promotion from assistant to associate professor accompanies the granting of tenure. When policy and procedure pertaining to tenure and promotion are readily available and clearly understood, most related disputes can be prevented from taking on large proportions. This is so because when tenure is denied, and it becomes evident that the decision was not discriminatory, arbitrary, or capricious, then the issue is whether the institution had a policy and followed it. When it is self-evident that internal policies and procedures have been followed, fewer negative decisions are contested, and those that are can be addressed more effectively in the appeal and grievance processes, as well as in litigation. Unfortunately, tenure is an either/or proposition and there is not much room for other alternatives to resolution of disputes resulting from denial of it.

As a matter of practice, the more complicated tenure and promotion policy and procedure are, the more difficult they are to follow without violating them. Some violations matter more than others, and a key question attached to many appeals, grievances, and lawsuits is, "Was a given departure from written policy and procedure sufficient to affect the outcome?"

If the answer is yes, then the institution will lose its case unless corrective action is taken. If the answer is no, the institution and its agents will still be hard pressed to make their case as respondents to a grievance or defendants in litigation and will look bad even if they win in court. Thus, it is critical for the institution to have clear policy and follow it. Any good tenure and promotion policy has two primary goals: to ensure fairness to the candidate and to protect academic standards. At this point, one can see that good policy is a tool, not an impediment, in making hard decisions regarding tenure and promotion and following through with them successfully.

In instances where the dean or provost determines that procedure has not been followed, they have an opportunity early on to make a key decision. Do they allow someone to be tenured who perhaps does not deserve it on the merits of their work, or do they try to deny tenure and/or promotion and attempt to defend their decision in a grievance or in court? Or do they look for another approach? The right answer is that another approach should be sought, and it is not difficult to do.

The best way to handle most of these situations is to identify the points of departure from policy and procedure, clarify any ambiguities that exist regarding those policies, and send the matter back to the beginning of the decision-making process to be done over. This must be done without drawing or implying any conclusions *a priori*. The problem may lie anywhere along the process, but in most instances it has roots in how the department head or chair managed assembly of materials and consideration by the faculty. The sooner breaches of policy and procedure can be identified and corrected, the more likely is the restoration of integrity to the outcome.

This point raises the necessity of ensuring that all department heads or chairs are thoroughly grounded in policy and procedure and imbued with a sense of urgency about following it meticulously. Similarly, deans must be held accountable for ensuring that policy and procedure are followed and for preventing recommendations to come forward that may be flawed by procedural error.

Another facet of tenure and promotion that is closely tied to prevention of future conflict is granting tenure to assistant professors who have not shown sufficient progress to warrant concomitant promotion to associate professor. This should be prohibited by policy with an allowance for rare exceptions subject to the approval of the chief academic officer. In research universities and in most postsecondary environments, individuals who do not rise to a level of productivity sufficient to warrant promotion at the time of the tenure decision are likely to be marginal for the rest of their careers, at least in their current environment. They will habitually be at the bottom of the annual evaluation and salary adjustment process and may feel a growing sense of second-class citizenship, burnout, and resentment.

POST-TENURE REVIEW

Many institutions now have a system for reviewing the productivity of faculty members throughout their careers following the granting of tenure. These fall into two basic categories: cyclical or triggered. Cyclical systems review the productivity of all faculty members at a prescribed interval. This usually involves suggestions for career development, nudging driftwood, and, rarely, cutting out deadwood. Triggered systems are based on a thoroughgoing annual evaluation and are triggered on a case-by-case basis by documentation of poor performance. In both instances, the first objective is to ensure that faculty careers stay on track and that the institution is well served. However, any evaluation system has the potential to inspire conflict. Since post-tenure review can lead to dismissal of a tenured faculty member, the level of conflict can escalate quickly and involve a lot of people, including those that see the process as threatening tenure as an institution. It is self-evident that allowing chronic low productivity in a few individuals, while their colleagues carry an extra load as a result, also breeds resentment and conflict.

Whether cyclical or triggered, the policies and procedures governing post-tenure review must be clear. Inevitably, they become interactive with other policies, such as those controlling annual evaluation and gender and racial discrimination.

APPEAL AND GRIEVANCE

Appeal and grievance were discussed in Chapter 3 and are included here in terms of implementation within the context of other relevant policies and procedures. An appeal is a key step in due process that precedes a grievance. In most instances, this goes to the department head or chair, then to the dean, and finally to the chief academic officer. If the matter is not resolved at that level, the complainant has access to an internal grievance, most commonly conducted by a panel of peers who make recommendations to the president or chancellor. It is absolutely essential that the policy guiding these processes be clear and accessible, and that the administrative practices attending them are part of the collective understanding of the institution.

The orderly conduct of dispute resolution requires that, if not resolved informally, complaints must be reviewed at each relevant administrative level. This is also a prerequisite to grievances within the institution and external litigation. Appeals must be governed by clear policy and universally understood practice. For example, the appeal must be made in writing, stating the complaint and the relief sought. After an independent investigation based on a review of the record, the responsible administrator must produce a finding within a specific period of time.

Most systems hold the appeal process as the last opportunity to settle the dispute prior to the onset of litigation. In most instances, a formal campus-level grievance involves attorneys, either as participants or advisors. This is not the case in administrative appeals, although they may be on the sidelines advising the appellant and respondents from a greater distance. For example, the complainant's attorney may have written the appeal. A university attorney almost surely will look at a draft of the administrative finding.

It is essential that the appeal process allow for enough discretion that the responsible administrator can watch for opportunities to correct errors in procedure when an all or none outcome is required, such as in a tenure denial, or access alternatives to resolve conflict that underlies the dispute at hand. For example, a department chair may be appealing a poor evaluation by the dean to the chief academic officer (CAO). The department chair believes that the poor evaluation is an antecedent to being relieved of her administrative responsibilities, which might well derail her career plans. The CAO may have learned during the review (or may have already known) that the dean and this particular department chair have a history of not getting along. For lack of a more definitive diagnosis, one might suggest that their personalities conflict, and the interpersonal chemistry is bad. If they both took a personality test, it might turn out that their characteristics are not a good match. The dispute over the evaluation might be symptomatic of this, or it might actually indicate poor performance, although the poor performance might stem from the chronic tensions between the chair and the dean. Binding arbitration, mediation, and facilitation of the relationship all are possible resources the CAO might want to call on as part of the outcome of the appeal if it seems that both of the parties have the talent and ability to do excellent work.

Sexual Harassment and Racial and Gender Discrimination

Every institution has a policy on sexual harassment and racial and gender discrimination, and it is sure to have been tested many times. The issue here is to place these policies in the context of others. For example, if policy and procedure for annual evaluation, promotion, and tenure are not clear, then it is much harder to address questions about whether poor evaluations or denial of tenure or promotion were the result of poor performance or racial or gender discrimination.

In instances of sexual harassment and gender or racial discrimination that become affirmative action complaints, it is critical for the policies of the Office of Affirmative Action, by whatever name, to be crystal clear. For example, it should be evident that these officers adjudicate; they do not advocate, at least not for individuals. It must be clear whether they confine their intervention to those cases that meet the legal standard of harassment or discrimination. If so, they must take an active role in steering other problem situations to appropriate alternative pathways to resolution.

Affirmative action officers must be interactive with ombudspersons, the mediation system, advocacy offices for women and people of color, and administrators generally. They must have ready access to all policies that are commonly relevant to disputes. They must have access to competent legal advice. They must be part of an integrated system of DPRM without compromising their ability to adjudicate instances of actual racial and gender discrimination.

ACCESSIBILITY

The best policy is of no value if those who depend upon it, or are required to follow it, do not know about it or do not understand it. This means that the faculty and staff must know where to go for this information. Such points of access must be widely known and easy to find. The policy must be readily understandable. Common means of providing access to policy include web sites and handbooks.

While all employees must be conversant in how to access this system, some must know it chapter and verse. Prominent among these are the chief academic officer, deans, department heads and chairs, affirmative action officers, and ombudspersons. All too often administrators fall into the trap of bridling at "all this bureaucracy" and fail to stay abreast of policy. Given the relatively short tenure of people in such offices, turnover creates additional requirements for training and orientation programs designed to make certain that line administrators know all relevant policy or, more realistically, know where to find it and can locate it when necessary. Following established policy and procedure makes administrators more effective, raises their credibility immeasurably, and allows them to be more productive because they spend less time putting out fires caused by failure to follow policy. Faculty and staff are also more productive and enjoy coming to work because they know where they stand and how their world of work operates. They have greater confidence in and respect for their supervisors. It is essential for everyone to have equal and ready access to policy and a common understanding of what it means. The watchword is KISS—keep it simple, stupid.

CULTURAL AND STRUCTURAL CONTEXT: GOVERNANCE AND POLICY

Policy is created, updated, and implemented within a governance context. Governance itself is a source of conflict, frequently over policy. This can be very productive. The elements of governance are the central administration, the deans, and the faculty council by whatever name. When the institution has a contract with a union or bargaining unit, that entity is also part of governance. The role of unions varies and affects the strength of the faculty senate or council and the relationship between it and the central administration. When a union has an operational presence on a campus, many aspects of conflict resolution, or at least the policies that guide them, may be subsumed in the contract.

All the stakeholders, either directly or through their representatives, need to have a role in policy development. Most commonly, the chief academic officer will represent the institution in working with the deans and the faculty council, by whatever name. In smaller institutions, the president may take a more direct role. Other vice presidents will be involved to a greater or lesser extent, and their roles will reflect whether or not the so-called faculty council includes other unclassified professional staff.

The governing board can mandate policy or mandate that the institution(s) under its jurisdiction develop a policy for its approval. The latter is the best approach whenever possible. Policy changes can be initiated by the faculty council or the administration but are best developed collaboratively. This can become a rigorous process depending on how much change is involved. However, when the faculty and the administration go at it on policy development, under the oversight of the board, special interests tend to be winnowed out, and the good of the institution is most likely to prevail.

It is essential that the authority of the president or chancellor be preserved in this process. One of the best ways to preserve authority is to use it sparingly. The underlying logic of new or altered policy should be strong enough to create a consensus. Often, policies that result in significant change, such as the creation of post-tenure review, are initiated by a mandate from the board, the president, or the chief academic officer. Exactly what that policy says and what its impact will be will result from an iterative process that is circulated among the central administration, the faculty governing body, and the deans until it reaches a functional level.

Colleges and universities are process-driven institutions. The process of policy development is key to successful development of an effective system of conflict prevention and resolution. It also can be an instrument for bringing the institution together with greater productivity in academic work because of a higher level of trust among the players, including individual faculty.

All this takes time. Much of this time is spent in meetings, consuming the time and talent of significant numbers of people. This can be mitigated by ensuring that issues and ideas are chosen carefully, and only those issues which stand to be important to many over time are pursued at all. Efficiency of effort is essential, including the ability of committee chairs and task forces to run effective and productive meetings. This requires that effective people become involved in shared governance, that a value is placed on their work, and that they are rewarded for doing it well. This raises the concept of the scholarship of service and the scholarship of administration.

SERVICE AND ADMINISTRATION
AS SCHOLARLY WORK

The standard model of academic work has been for the words *research* and *scholarship* to be interchangeable. Strict criteria and standards for quality research and creative work have been established in the various disciplines. This is the heart and soul of institutions of higher education. But it is too confining. The standard model has also allowed for the criteria used to determine quality in discipline-based work to stop at the borders of the discipline. Service work, such as participating on task forces to establish policy important to the institution, has received short shrift. People who work hard at it and do it well tend to do so out of a sense of personal interest or altruism. All too often, they are neither evaluated nor rewarded for it.

There can also be a tendency to do poor work in service to the institution. Meetings drag on and proceed from one to the next without syntax or results. Politics creep into the discourse and, all too often, into the results. No scholar of repute would allow this in the conduct of her research. So why allow it in the conduct of institutional service?

In the early 1990s, Boyer laid the groundwork for correcting this state of affairs. As president of the Carnegie Foundation, Boyer published the seminal work *Scholarship Reconsidered: Priorities of the Professoriate* (1990), which redesigned the vernacular for thinking about, evaluating, and rewarding scholarship. Boyer framed his premise on four types of scholarship: discovery, integration, application, and teaching. Variations on the theme have emerged, but Boyer's basic construct provided the tools for allowing institutions to create more flexible models for engaging individual strengths. It also raised the possibility of placing a value on service (including community engagement) and rewarding it.

To accomplish this in a more definitive way, a workable means of evaluation and reward was needed. This was addressed, at least in part, by the subsequent work of Glassick, Huber, and Maeroff (1997), which elucidates six criteria for evaluating scholarly work in research, teaching, and service. These criteria serve very well for any discipline.

1) Clear goals

2) Adequate preparation

3) Appropriate methods

4) Significant results

5) Effective presentation

6) Reflective critique

Few would argue with the value of these criteria in assessing research and creative work. It has become ever more evident that they also provide a better basis for the assessment and reward of teaching. They can be effective in the assessment and rewarding of service, including service to the institution.

For example, if the conduct of a task force or committee on any subject, be it curriculum or policy development, were measured against these criteria, the quality of the work would go up. Efficiency would also increase, and politics would be marginalized or excluded. Who, after all, would allow politics to taint their scholarship? Furthermore, to the extent an institution establishes scholarly criteria and standards to evaluate service, faculty members who make major contributions to that area can be properly rewarded.

In an environment of shared governance, faculty, staff, and administrators are collaborating to create the best product to serve the institution. This includes the general faculty, faculty and staff leadership, deans, and central administration. There is nothing in this approach that undermines the authority of the administration. Authority is not the issue. Ideas are the issue, and frequently collaboration is a prerequisite for developing the best ideas. As part of this process, the same criteria for assessment of scholarship apply to administrative roles as apply to service work on the part of the faculty and staff.

The resultant increase in quality of policy, and the enhanced feeling of collaboration in its development, will contribute to a reduction in the institutional tendency toward unproductive conflict.

5 ◆ The Players and Their Roles: Governance and Administration

The Board

The governing board, whether its members are called regents, curators, trustees, or visitors, has many roles, depending on the size of the institution, its mission, and whether it is public or private. Members of boards of public institutions are elected in some instances or appointed by the governor and confirmed by a legislative body in others. Commonly, individual institutions have their own governing boards and this is, of course, the standard model for private colleges and universities. By contrast, one governing board may have authority over multiple campuses of one university. In some instances, they will preside over a system of several separate state-supported institutions. On balance, governing boards are responsible for establishing policy and holding the institutional president or chancellor accountable for seeing that his or her college or university adheres to it.

The board has the potential for conflict on a number of fronts. Common examples would include disputes with state government (for public-supported institutions), with an institutional chief executive officer (CEO), with the faculty as a represented body, with the students as a represented body, or with members of its own staff, not to mention each other. Conflict with a CEO likely will have to do with that individual's personal performance. Disputes with the other groups will most likely be based on budget or policy development. However, the primary interest of this discussion is in disputes that arise on institutional campuses and the role the board and its agents play in their prevention or resolution.

As a general rule, governing boards should not become entangled in disputes involving individuals or warring factions on a campus. They should, however, ensure that the institution(s) under their control has effective policies and procedures for addressing them and that they are properly implemented. Exceptions do exist. One would be the possible role of the board in final review of cases involving dismissal of tenured faculty.

The best place for disputes to be resolved is as close to the source as possible. Direct involvement of the governing board in disputes involving individuals or groups on an individual campus violates this principle. The need for the board to become engaged would be a sure sign that the institution does not have appropriate policy or procedures for dealing with such problems, or that the campus leadership is not addressing such issues effectively, or both.

Chris Townes is the chair of the governing board of Upstate University and CEO of his own large real estate development company. He receives a call from a very angry and persistent man that pulls him away from an important business conference. Townes is in the final stages of arranging financing on a new shopping mall and has six of his top people holed up in the conference room running the numbers. The voice on the other end of the line is strained and crackles with suppressed anger. "Mr. Townes," the voice says, " I appreciate you taking my call. My name is Dan Boemer. I am a dentist in Troy, down in the southeast corner of the state."

Now that he has Townes's attention, Boemer keeps rolling breathlessly along. "Normally, I wouldn't bother you, but I have a major problem with Upstate University and their nursing program. My daughter has a 3.6 GPA and she was not admitted, if you can believe that. Her mother and I have to know what's going on. I absolutely cannot get a straight answer out of anyone up there, and I must have talked to half a dozen people. I've talked to that life sciences dean 'til I'm blue in the face and to tell you the truth, I've never been treated with such condescension. Ever."

There is a momentary break in Boemer's stream of consciousness, long enough for Townes, who desperately needs to get back to his $5,000 per hour meeting, to get a word in.

Townes has choices here. He can point out that he is a busy man and that these matters are handled elsewhere, refer the caller to the university president or to the executive officer of the board's staff, and forget it. He can tell the concerned father that he is busy now, but will get back to him. He can ask the father to write up his concerns and send him an email or letter describing the problem. He can ask his secretary to call the dean of life sciences at Upstate University with instructions to call Townes the next morning with an explanation. The list goes on. However, as it turns out, he takes a constructive path. His business experience has made him well equipped to deal with situations like this.

"Dr. Boemer," he said, "your concern is important to the board, and I appreciate your call. We have to keep in touch with what happens on our campuses, and we have to be sure people are being treated fairly—and respectfully, for that matter. Having said that, the people with the relevant information and responsibility to handle issues like this are on the campus. I would ask that you call Tom Sanford, the president at Upstate, and lay this out for him. Better yet, you might want to sketch it out in a letter or email, and then give him a call. For my part, before the day is over, I will call him and tell him about our conversation and let him know you will be contacting him."

There was a pause and Townes could sense that Dr. Boemer was thinking this over. "That's fair enough," Boemer replied. "I know you're very busy. I appreciate your taking time to talk to me. I will make some notes and fax them to President Sanford, then give him a call."

Any number of outcomes might result from this exchange, but with Townes's promise to call the Upstate president in advance, Dr. Boemer knows that his concerns are not being brushed aside. If everyone treats his case objectively and nondefensively from here on, the problem is likely to be resolved appropriately, even if not to everyone's liking. The central point is that if the right steps are taken at the outset, everyone has a much greater opportunity to reach resolution than if feelings are bruised further. Most likely, Mr. Townes will be curious about the dean's style. This is an opportunity to nip a problem in the bud, touch base with the institution's president, and learn a little more about the atmosphere and operating style of the institution without micromanaging it from his position on the board. It will take a little of his time. But if he is not willing to devote time to being a regent, he should not have taken on the responsibility.

The governing board should maintain the chain of command and hold its campus officers accountable, but also be knowledgeable of and have a feel for the campus climate and the style and effectiveness of its agents. A functional, minimalistic feedback loop among the various aspects of the campus and the governing board can benefit everyone.

THE PRESIDENT OR CHANCELLOR

System or multi-campus presidents and chancellors are not addressed per se in this discussion because everything that has been said about governing boards, with respect to conflict and disputes on campus, generally can be said about them. However, the chief executive officer (CEO) of the individual institution plays a key role in dispute resolution, management, and prevention (DRMP). This is not because he is involved day to day, but because the leadership sets the tone and, even more importantly, appoints the people who have primary responsibility for ensuring effectiveness in this area. Ultimately, the president is responsible for establishment and implementation of a system of DRMP that serves the institution's interests. This is done through leadership and management of personnel and by personal example.

The CEO is also responsible for issues beyond DRMP policy that have a direct impact on the degree of unproductive conflict experienced by the institution. She must hold her executive officers accountable for ensuring effective personnel management, including dispute resolution. These goals are achievable only through development of sound policy and systematic, sustained professional development of administrators. If the chancellor, her executive team, and the deans treat people with respect, share information openly, and seek input and advice, people will respond in kind. It is essential that department chairs and heads adopt this approach as well.

The CEO must maintain the integrity of the chain of command in terms of authority and responsibility. On the other hand, a free flow of information and an effective means of give and take must exist among the CEO, the provost and other senior officers, and the leadership of the faculty and students. The best means of accomplishing this are through telephone communication and face-to-face conversation. The nuances surrounding most conflicts are too numerous and subtle to trust to email. Exchanges of memos tend to cause even more trouble, not less. Memo exchange as a tool for conflict resolution is counterproductive in virtually every instance, especially at the level of the CEO, university executives, and deans. Communication is a good example of how the administrative style of the institution's leadership creates an atmosphere that favors the prevention and resolution of conflict. A feedback loop and exchange of information is essential, but writing should be used only to document facts and to finalize outcomes, not for exchanging opinions or initial exploration of options.

The CEO often is required to walk a very fine line between knowing what is going on in a given situation and being sensitive to the fact that he may well become the final arbiter in a grievance process.

When Dr. Boemer called President Sanford at Upstate University, Boemer had done what he thought was a pretty good job of documenting the issues surrounding the denial of his daughter's admission to the School of Nursing. The president seemed like a nice guy; very accommodating and engaging.

"Look, Dr. Boemer," Sanford said after they had talked over the case, "If your daughter's GPA is, as you say, in the top one-third of the applicants, it is hard to explain why she was not admitted. And the dean's comment that if you really wanted to help your daughter get admitted, you might have helped her write a presentable application, does seem uncalled for. Having said that, I don't remember the dean being hard to work with, at least not in my experience."

"I appreciate your receptivity, Mr. President," Boemer replied. "I have to emphasize that time is an issue. Jennie has been invited to an out-of-state program and has to notify them next week if she is going to enroll. The problem for me is that the tuition will be four times as high, and I have three kids in college already. I pay one hell of a lot of taxes in this state, and I sure don't like the idea of paying out-of-state tuition somewhere else so my daughter can go to nursing school."

"I understand," Sanford said. "I'll take care of it. Give me a couple of days, and either the dean or I will get back to you."

By "I'll take care of it," President Sanford meant he would get right on it in light of the time problem. In Dr. Boemer's heightened state of hopefulness, he took this statement to mean that Sanford would see to it that his daughter is admitted to the School of Nursing. The president's first thought was to ask the provost to follow up on this and get back to him so they can get it resolved. The provost, however, was out of town attending a conference, so he called Dean Denise Miller instead.

"Hello, Denise," Sanford said. "What do you know about a nursing school applicant by the name of Jennie Boemer?"

"A lot," the dean replied. "It seems like I've spent about half my time the last week talking to her father. He's a dentist, as you may know. It's a sad case, really. Jennie is a very nice young woman and desperately wants to become a nurse."

"Well, then what's the problem? If her GPA is in the top third, she is a nice young woman and is that highly motivated, why not just admit her?"

Dean Miller could sense the aggravation in the president's voice. She also knew Dr. Boemer had called the chair of the board because he had copied her on his email to Sanford. "If that were the whole story," she replied, "that is just what would have happened. We have already oversubscribed the class from 70 to 75. The real problems, though, are the GPA issue and a very poorly written essay in her application package."

The dean went on to explain that while Jennie Boemer's overall GPA was in the upper third of the applicant pool, her GPA in the core required courses was in the bottom third, and her science grades were in the low end of those. When her composite score was added up, she ranked 97th among 116 applicants. While not all that bad, she was a long way below the cutoff. All this had been explained more than once to Dr. Boemer, but he just responded by criticizing the standards. Miller acknowledged that she had, in fact, told Jennie's father that if he really wanted to increase his daughter's chances of admission he should have helped her write a decent (she might even have said coherent) essay. She knew this was a mistake as soon as she said it, but her frustration got the best of her. It was pretty clear, she thought to herself, that Boemer treated the president and the regent with more respect than he did her.

It was decided that Dean Miller would draft a letter to Dr. Boemer documenting the reasons why his daughter was not admitted to the nursing program. It was also decided that the dean would send the letter to Dr. Boemer, with a shown copy to the president and the regent. The letter included an apology for her "imprudent remark about helping your daughter with her essay which, of course, would have been unethical in any event." Although Miller did not say so, she was unhappy about being caught in the middle of the dispute that subsequently flared up when Boemer wrote a letter of complaint to the governor, his legislative representation, and the board of regents alleging that President Sanford had promised to admit his daughter to the School of Nursing and then reneged. He added that "apparently, the president cannot control his arrogant, condescending dean."

Even the most astute get caught at a busy moment and make a misstatement now and again. The whole episode could have been prevented if the president had substituted "I will look into it and call you back" for "I will take care of it." Some basic fact-finding would have put him in a position to end the dispute quickly. Hindsight is always perfect. It also should be noted that the dean did not help her own cause when she let her temper get away from her and made the snide remark to Dr. Boemer about his daughter's incoherent essay. One should never place weapons in the hands of one's adversaries and her remark did just that, putting Boemer in a position to criticize her to the president and regent, weakening her credibility. It may be the case that he was trying to bully her because of her gender. If so, that might make her comment understandable but it was poor strategy nonetheless. Also, given the emotional nature of the dispute and Dr. Boemer's persistence, it would have been a good idea to give the provost and president an early warning.

Taken individually, these are small incidents, but they can add up to create an atmosphere of communication and trust, or disorder and skepticism. Unproductive conflict is much less common in the former than in the latter.

THE CHIEF ACADEMIC OFFICER

The provost (or vice president for academic affairs) works in a triangulated environment marked by the president or chancellor, the faculty leadership (and the union if the campus has one), and the deans. Not to minimize the importance of the students, all other aspects of the institution encountered in the provost's work are subservient to these three. With regard to unproductive conflict within the institution, he has three basic areas of responsibility: 1) to be sure good policies, procedures, and practices exist and that they are accessible; 2) to be sure they are followed, up and down the chain of command; 3) to create and maintain a complete, integrated system of DPRM. Depending on institutional size and type, some of these responsibilities may be delegated to others or retained.

In theory, the chief academic officer (CAO) is responsible for academic policy. In practice, this means people and money. Mixing people and money with the spatula of academic freedom, in the transparent fishbowl of public scrutiny, makes conflict certain. Much of the conflict that takes place in this environment is productive and necessary, even invaluable. However, when it moves from conflict about ideas to conflict about or between personalities, resolution is required.

Colleges and universities are intended to exist for hundreds of years. They are expected to outlast even the most stable corporation. This is one reason people donate large sums of money to them in memory of themselves or a loved one. Posterity is an issue at an institution of higher learning. A major side effect of this is that change comes hard and, as a result, frustrations often run high. Both reasoned discourse and raw debate have important places in the elaboration of this idea. However, the resultant milieu can and does provide a seed bed for destructive conflict.

The most important organizing principle in this environment is process. If you think that should read vision, think again. Vision is essential, but without process, it can lead the institution into chaos. Having well-understood policies, procedures, and practices in place is absolutely essential to the success of the CAO and the institution. Policy, procedure, and practice comprise the canon law of the institution, and the CAO must be a canon lawyer. He must be aggressive in asserting that the deans and department heads or chairs adhere to policy. Failure to follow the canon law creates a lack of confidence and, eventually, a lack of trust, in the institutional leadership. It also is the most common reason for litigation. When a college or university loses a lawsuit, it usually is because of a breach of its own policy.

If the CAO does not demand that her subordinates follow policy and established procedure, she will quickly find herself expending an inordinate amount of time, effort, and intellectual energy attempting to adjudicate disputes in which the appropriate outcome is negated by procedural error.

Following good policy and procedure must go hand in hand with actions that, on their face, pass the test of basic fairness. The question is, "Fairness to whom?" Certainly fairness is due the appellant or grievant, but also the respondent, colleagues, and other internal stakeholders, taxpayers, and tuition payers.

The basis of fairness is fact-finding. The reason for this is that truth can only be defined by knowing all the facts, and fairness without truth is an illusion. The provost encounters innumerable opportunities to jump to conclusions, to take accusations at face value, and to commit too quickly to a position. Then, upon learning more, she will have to reverse course and come off looking indecisive or wishy-washy.

Amber Ellinwood, provost of Downstate University for about 18 months, knew about the denial of Albert Fine's tenure in the Department of Chemistry because she had reviewed the file and endorsed the decision. This was a couple of weeks before the phone call from Jack Foster, one of the university ombudsmen. Jack arranged for Dr. Fine and himself to meet with Ellinwood prior to submitting a written appeal. University policy required that if the aggrieved party wished to appeal, it must be in writing. Following a written appeal and decision, a grievance hearing would be convened if the matter were not resolved to the satisfaction of the appellant. Amber was a little uncomfortable with this arrangement because she was automatically put in the position of reviewing a decision she had recently endorsed.

Ombudsman Foster was a long-time employee of Downstate University. An associate professor of agronomy, he had served numerous terms as a faculty senator and was a productive scholar in teaching and research. He knew a lot about how Downstate worked. "Provost Ellinwood," he said in his gravelly voice, "as you know, my role is not as an advocate for either Dr. Fine or the university, but to assist the faculty member in making certain that his appeal is properly prepared and heard. I thought it might be beneficial if we went over the process and timeline, just to be sure we all understand things the same. I also think there might be a point or two about the case that ought to be discussed before going further."

Ellinwood smelled trouble. The "point or two" sounded like a reference to a surprise, something she liked to avoid. She placed the legal pad she had been holding on the edge of the table and gave Dr. Fine her full attention. "Let's start," she said, "by hearing any questions you have about the process and any issues you think ought to be discussed before you write your appeal."

Fine shifted around in his chair and glanced out the window. He obviously was ill at ease, but who wouldn't be under the circumstances. "I think the policy and procedure for an appeal are pretty clear," he said. "What I really would like to discuss is what I think are improprieties in how the process was carried out."

Amber took a deep breath and mulled this over. No irregularities had been mentioned before. The faculty in Fine's department had voted eleven to four against his tenure. Two more had voted for tenure, but against promotion to associate, which was moot because the university had a policy against tenure without promotion for assistant professors. The department head had, with some degree of waffling, recommended against tenure and promotion, as had the dean and his advisory committee. Their reasons were valid; Fine was a mediocre teacher showing some improvement and, as a chemist in a strong research department, had yet to attract outside money. Ellinwood recalled he had three publications, maybe four, one of which was from his dissertation.

"Let's be frank," she said. "You had a negative recommendation at every level of the process. Based on my review of your credentials and the criteria and standards of the Department of Chemistry, those recommendations were well founded. Up to this moment, no one has mentioned irregularities in the process. So what new information do you have?"

Fine hunched forward in his chair. He looked at the floor for a minute, then at Jack Foster. Leaning back and looking at the ceiling, he told the provost that two of the faculty who had supported him had come to him a week ago and said that although university policy and procedure prescribed a meeting of the faculty to discuss candidates for promotion and tenure, there had been none in his case. "Chemistry has a new head," he went on to say. "This is his first year. He is still getting his feet on the ground and may not have been aware of the procedure. I think he did send out my packet to the entire tenured faculty and got a letter from each of them along with their vote. As I got to looking into it further with Professor Foster's help, I found that two of my reference letters were distributed a week after the original packet and by that time some of the faculty already had sent in their letter and vote."

"You can see the problem," Foster interjected. "Without the faculty meeting, Dr. Fine's supporters never had an opportunity to point out to the rest of the faculty what they viewed his strengths to be. The letters are a separate issue. Maybe they are of less importance, maybe not, but university policy requires letters of reference, so it would seem that they all ought to be considered."

He was right, of course. Ellinwood thought this through, tapping her ballpoint pen on the edge of the coffee table. If Fine appealed based on the premise they were discussing, and she denied it, and it went directly to civil court (which would not happen), the university might or might not win the case aided by the doctrine of substantial compliance. This simply meant that the court might find that the university had made a good faith effort to conduct an impartial process and its breach of procedure was not significant enough to have affected the outcome. Fine's performance was way below the standards of the department and the university and that was why the faculty voted the way they did. Even so, if it went to a general grievance panel in the university, they were sure to reverse her based on the valid premise that the university had not followed its own policy and the process looked unfair on its face. Then, because of a procedural error, they would have a newly tenured faculty member who was underqualified. Upholding the appeal would result in the same outcome, just for a different reason. Along with everything else, she knew she needed to speed up her plans for a new department head orientation and training program.

"I appreciate the opportunity to discuss this," she said. "I would suggest that Dr. Fine go ahead and write a letter of appeal and that we proceed in the usual manner. These procedural issues will be in the letter, of course."

When she reached the point in the appeal process of interviewing the dean and department head, she learned that the dean had only found out about this problem when contacted by Ellinwood about the appeal. The department head had found out the proper procedure from talking to another head at a neighborhood potluck dinner, but when he reviewed it in the handbook, he didn't see it as being of decisive importance, so let it go. "Having read the letters each faculty member wrote on this," he said, "it was clear to me that a meeting would not have changed anything so I didn't worry about it."

Ellinwood wanted to pound her forehead on the table. "Lawyers call that notion the doctrine of substantial compliance," she said, her frustration showing through. "Even if it happens to be valid, it plays a lot better in court than it does on campus. When you don't follow established procedure, especially in a controversial situation, you are going to throw fuel on the fire every time. For future reference."

Being blessed with a full share of common sense, Ellinwood made a good decision. She called time out. Her response to Professor Fine's appeal was that procedural errors had indeed taken place and that they were of sufficient magnitude that a reasonable person might believe that they could have influenced the outcome. On the other hand, the evaluation of the faculty and others as to the substance of his candidacy could not be summarily dismissed. Thus, she was sending his packet back to the department with a prescriptive letter to the dean stating each step that was to be followed in conducting the entire process again. This included a faculty meeting to discuss Fine's case. The results were exactly the same, except that the two faculty members who had voted for tenure but not promotion the first time, now voted against tenure because they had since learned their first position was not an option.

She invited Dr. Fine to her office to give him the letter denying his appeal, based on the outcome of the new process. Professor Foster came along. Fine seemed disappointed but not surprised. As he got up to leave, she asked "Are you proud of your work at this university?"

At first he didn't answer. When he got to the door, he turned and looked at her. "Not especially," he said. Dr. Fine did not apply for a grievance hearing.

THE DEAN

The dean is the chief administrative officer for the college or school, be it all organized around one discipline, or a collage of them, as in Colleges of Arts and Sciences. There is one very large difference between arts and sciences and professional programs like engineering or business. Instead of being comprised of one general cultural makeup, such colleges tend to be very large, consisting of many different cultures. Mathematicians are as different from political scientists as engineers are from agronomists. The biological and physical sciences comprise the haves, and everyone else the have-nots. These differences present a large array of problems and opportunities that make these colleges especially demanding to lead. The complexity goes down, of course, when these units are split into a liberal arts college and a science college.

The match between the personality and style of the dean and the collective culture of the college is absolutely critical to the prevention, resolution, and management of unproductive conflict. The ability to channel conflict along productive lines is a special attribute that some deans possess and others do not. This characteristic can be the difference between success and failure.

The role of the dean in DPRM has much to do with the administrative structure of the college, more precisely with the role of department heads and chairs. With a rotating chair system, much of the power for any real decision-making is kept in the hands of the dean. This means the dean is more likely to be on, or close to, the frontlines in instances of conflict among faculty members, and has more leverage over the disposition of resources in the department. One obvious result of such an arrangement is that a greater proportion of conflict is going to involve the dean directly. When appointed heads or chairs are the norm (assuming an appropriate faculty role in their selection and retention) they (should) have more authority and responsibility, leaving the dean in a better position to be a fundraiser, planning leader, direction setter, and adjudicator when needed. It also means the department heads and chairs had better be trained and educated in their work and held to a high standard of administrative performance.

Like the CAO, the dean must know and follow policy and procedure scrupulously. Energetic, motivated individuals who come to these jobs with expectations of high achievement can find this to be bureaucratic and frustrating, at least initially. This can create a lot of conflict in a hurry because it leads to rapid change, which many will oppose, with concomitant failure to consult adequately and follow procedure and practice. In the long run more progress can be made in less time in a university setting by engaging stakeholders. This deprives no one of their ultimate decision-making authority, leads to better decisions, reduces time and effort, and minimizes drainage of intellectual energy. It should be noted that if deans view their present position as a steppingstone, the dangers associated with change go up.

In universities, the dean works in a triangulated environment comprised of faculty, department heads and chairs, and the provost. On occasion, students, the president, and outside constituents introduce themselves into the core relationship, but most situations are worked out through faculty, department heads and chairs, and the CAO.

Central to the dean's success in dispute resolution are good people skills that inspire confidence, listening skills, an innovative eye for opportunities, and a sense of humor. The dean's motives for consultation also are important. If one consults with the faculty or their representatives so he can say he did so, but without really listening, hearing, and respecting their views, an opportunity is lost and a problem is created. The lost opportunity is missing the chance to get some really great ideas into play. Most faculty members are very smart, innovative people. They bring a lot of knowledge to the table. The problem created is the perception that the dean listens but does not hear, or that he is dismissive or condescending. Listening without hearing comes to be viewed as disingenuous, which contributes to an atmosphere of distrust and creates a breeding ground for conflict.

The dean *cannot* automatically back the department head or chair. Every issue must be assessed objectively. All administrators are expected to support the people who report to them. However, the proper definition of support, that lends itself to resolution of disputes early in their development, is that the dean helps the department head or chair solve problems. It does not mean that the dean indiscriminately backs up the head's decisions and actions.

THE DEPARTMENT HEAD OR CHAIR

The semantic exercise of trying to differentiate between heads and chairs can be pretty pointless. The real issue is whether the person in the role serves at the pleasure of the dean, has real authority and responsibility, and undergoes continuous professional development in administration, or whether the individual is, for all practical purposes, elected for a rotating term, has limited administrative responsibility and authority, and is less subject to the authority of the dean. The latter arrangement can work in mature departments in mature institutions, until the personalities change with turnover. But where experience and real problem solving are required, such as in the resolution of disputes, the responsibility passes to the dean. The disadvantage of this arrangement is that the success of all conflict resolution in the college rests primarily on one person and is subject to the ability of that individual. With the right dean in a small college, this can work until the dean departs. However, spreading the responsibility out over several able people is more likely to be successful over the long haul.

If the chair is the first person involved in resolution of disputes in a department, issues are addressed in a more timely manner by someone who should know much more about the nuances of the problem and the disputants. When the department head is the subject of, or a party to, the dispute and the parties are unable to resolve the matter themselves, the dean is the right person to take a role in creating an environment in which the issue can be addressed.

Of greatest importance is the role of the department chair in creating an environment that allows for productive conflict, raw debate, and reasoned discourse, but mitigates unproductive conflict and disputes. She can do this through the allocation of work, the annual goal setting and evaluation and reward process, and also by adding the right personal touch day to day. For this to work well, the head must know the strengths, weaknesses, and aspirations of every member of her faculty. She must optimize individual strengths and minimize individual weaknesses in the setting of goals and the allocation of effort. In this way, individual faculty members can be successful and the department can advance collectively—farther and faster than if part of the faculty were burned out and wasting their time. Because everyone is (and feels) valued, unproductive conflict is less likely to occur and is easier to overcome. Only an able head or chair that has a passion for the job and wants to serve in that way can do this well. A mediocre, unimaginative leader cannot, and a personnel committee cannot.

It should be noted that a free flow of communication among these officers is essential. It is important to observe the chain of command, but not so that opportunities to solve problems quickly are missed.

6 ♦ THE PLAYERS AND THEIR ROLES: INSTITUTIONAL OFFICES

The individual players who have key roles in dispute prevention, resolution, and management (DPRM) must be part of a coherent system. Other key aspects of that system are offices within the institution that provide service of various kinds to support those who have complaints and concerns and those who are responsible for resolving them. There are many institutional variations for each. As we shall see in Chapter 8, they all must work as a coherent whole to optimize the institution's ability to manage unproductive conflict in the most effective manner possible.

OMBUDSPERSONS

The term *ombudsperson* is used here in the narrow sense of a service by a person, not the maintenance of an office with multiple services. The ombudsperson is not an advocate, but rather someone that understands the problem solving and adjudication system in the institution and helps individual employees find their way through it as effectively as possible. The ombudsperson is there to help find solutions to problems, or at least to help concerned parties identify options to pursue. In some institutions, the Office of the Ombudsman (by whatever specific name) furthers this role by informal mediation and facilitation, at least at some level. Sometimes this office includes an array of dispute resolution options and serves students as well as faculty and staff. A survey of college and university web sites will reveal any number of examples of organizational structure.

Several considerations become important in determining how best to structure ombudsman service and its relationship to other components of a dispute resolution system.

Issues arising among faculty, staff, and administration differ markedly from those encountered by students. More importantly, the context within which they must be resolved is very different. Guidelines and procedures in most student handbooks, for example, would fall far short of those required to address disputes among faculty or between faculty and administrators. Further, personnel who are highly effective in a student affairs environment may not resonate with the issues that lead to conflict involving faculty and professional staff. The reverse is equally true. The obvious exception, of course, is conflict between faculty and students. Faculty-student conflict is generally short lived because of the duration of any given course. Future relationships tend not to be affected except in extreme situations. This does not apply to the relationship between a graduate student and his major professor. Thus, there is much to be said for having a separate ombudsperson system for faculty and professional staff.

Ombudspersons lose their effectiveness in two ways: loose lips and accumulated baggage. Most of the baggage comes from allowing themselves to slide into the role of advocate. They must know how the institution works and be respected by their peers, both for their own work history and, most importantly, for their personal integrity and reliability. Among the reliability issues, confidentiality is most important. Ombudspersons who are employed full-time for several years may lose their effectiveness, but they will be very difficult to replace. Because of difficulty in terminating their employment, the institution might find itself reassigning them and hiring a new ombudsperson, adding on more people unnecessarily.

This dilemma can be avoided, and excellent service provided at a far lower cost, by appointing ombudspersons from the faculty and staff on a part-time, or overload, basis for a specific term. However, this approach does raise the question of whether ombudspersons are creatures of the administration and, therefore, suspect. It can be easily solved by having them appointed by the president of the faculty senate or equivalent, in consultation with the chief academic officer, instead of the other way around. Even though their stipend comes from university funds, they will be seen as the independent operators they are with this selection process.

It is essential that ombudspersons be thoroughly grounded in institutional policy and procedure, as well as all the avenues for addressing problems, regardless of their nature. Thus, an organized training program must be in place to ensure they are prepared to serve effectively.

MEDIATORS

Mediation is a process whereby the disputants agree to find a resolution to their dispute with the assistance of a neutral third party, the mediator. Mediation has been described in Chapter 3. It suffices here to comment on the mediators themselves.

Anyone can be a mediator at some level. Some individuals come to it naturally. Training raises the skill level and creates an understanding of how mediation fits into an integrated system of dispute resolution. Certification simply documents that an individual has received training and attained a minimal level of competence. Mediation training is valuable to anyone involved in dispute resolution, even if they never become a certified mediator.

While the institution can hire certified mediators, or have existing staff trained and certified, the best approach is to use outsiders on a contract basis. A list of certified mediators can be created and drawn from on a case-by-case basis. There are several advantages to this approach.

It is essential that the mediator have no existing or potential authority over either disputant. This can be addressed by using an outside mediator. Since mediation requires complete disclosure, candor, and exploration of solutions, the parties must have absolute confidence that the content of the mediation will never find its way into the rumor mill or the institution's collective memory bank. This can be best accomplished by outside mediators.

The caseload is impossible to predict. With outside mediators, the efficiency of cost and effect is one for one. Also, if any specific mediator proves not to be effective, their services simply are not called upon again.

The use of outside mediators requires that someone within the institution be designated the responsibility for maintaining the list of approved mediators and organizing the logistics of each mediation. However, the organizational responsibility is going to be necessary whether the mediator(s) is internal or external. Any institution includes numerous individuals with the skill set to organize the mediation service. Obviously, the requisite skills must include a commitment to confidentiality.

THE OFFICE OF AFFIRMATIVE ACTION

By whatever name, the Office of Affirmative Action (OAA) or its equivalent has a unique and important role. Such offices are not instruments of government. They are an office of the institution, staffed by institutional employees charged with ensuring that a level playing field is maintained regardless of race, gender, national origin, disability, Vietnam era status, or sexual orientation (the latter not being universal in policy) and that state and federal regulations and institutional policies are followed.

These officers must match the institution and the demands of the job. The nature of the mission of the OAA ensures that the office will deal with volatile issues and emotional people. Baggage piles up quickly. Some people have the personality and style, as well as the work ethic, to deal with the baggage as they go. Others do not, and trouble accumulates rapidly around them.

Whatever else might be included in the OAA mission in a given institution, adjudication of complaints brought by individuals or groups about racial and gender discrimination is paramount. Advocacy for a principle, for example, the institutional need to act affirmatively in advancing the role and standing of women and people of color, is not in conflict with the primary role of adjudicating complaints. Advocacy for individuals, however, is in clear contradiction to the adjudication role because conflicts of interest become inevitable. Sooner or later, the OAA will be called upon to adjudicate a matter involving an individual it has previously advocated for. As time goes by, the number of such instances will increase. Thus, it is important to keep advocacy for individuals and adjudication in separate hands.

As part of advocating a principle, the OAA can and must educate the institutional community on recruiting and hiring strategies and retention issues. It is critical that OAA, the faculty leadership (and union, if one is involved), and the administration are on the same page in terms of law, policy, strategy, and overarching philosophy. Some of the most ferocious conflicts have their roots in complaints to the OAA.

Two primary sets of dynamics contribute to tensions in this area. One is that those bringing complaints tend to hold the opinion that the OAA and the administration are too easygoing with offenders in the area of discrimination and harassment, while those complained against more commonly believe they are the object of a witch-hunt. Individuals who inform about harassing situations, but want, or say they want, no action taken, create another complicating dynamic. The following example gives insight into how this happens.

Matt Rivers was interim chair of the Department of Civil Engineering. Jesse Small, who had served in the chair role for 15 years, had a stent installed to prop open a coronary artery two years after his quadruple bypass and stepped down six months ago. Matt's tenure as the new chair had been a baptism by fire, partly because he had inherited the same departmental environment that had caused Jesse's artery to close off in the first place. Today was no exception.

Willa Renfro, a third-year tenure-track assistant professor, had just left his office. Willa was extremely smart, with a National Science Foundation grant and five or six publications on new work. She struggled a little when teaching undergraduates, or so some said, but was getting better—or so some said. Matt was trying to get a better handle on that, especially since Willa's mid-probationary review was at hand. Her visit had left him a little off center.

"I've really been reluctant to talk to you about this," she had begun.

This inspired unease in Matt. He had been on the job long enough to know trouble when he saw it. Willa shifted in her chair. Arms folded, she looked down at her shoes.

"I want to tell you something," she went on, "but I don't want you to do anything, at least not now. Maybe I'm just being too sensitive."

Matt had an uneasy feeling that he knew what this was going to be about. "I can't promise that," he said, "but let's go ahead and see what the problem is. We can only deal with it if we get it on the table."

"Maria said I shouldn't say anything: that I ought to just tough it out until I get tenure, assuming I do."

Maria was the only other woman in a department of 18. She was tough, smart, and successful. Over time she had come to give as good as she got. Maria and Rivers got on pretty well. He knew she had had a few rough years, at least in the early going.

Willa paused, obviously distressed. Her hands were clenched. She had red blotches on her neck. Rivers thought she was going to cry. "I'm always on the margin," she was saying. "Every now and then it gets very rough. But mostly, they just don't think about what they are doing or saying." Rivers assumed "they" meant some or all of the men on the faculty. "But," she went on, "I can't take another day of John Haden."

She paused again. John Haden was an associate professor and had been for 20 years. Not that being a career associate professor is not an honorable estate, but it usually signified some kind of disconnect between the professor and the direction and standards of the department. Sometimes, it just reflected marginal productivity. Haden had been tenured as an assistant professor, something the university had long since discontinued, and had been one for six or eight years before being promoted. He could be a man of contradictions. In Rivers' opinion, he could be a real jerk.

The pause went on. "What is the problem with John?" he asked.

Willa took a deep breath. "Well, he always seems to wind up sitting by me at a meeting. Every now and then, he tells a very crude joke. I guess he's always done that, but I don't like it. A couple of times lately he looked right at me while he told a really gross, pretty explicit story. If he walks up to talk, he stands almost on top of me. It's very intimidating. And, at times, he stares at my breasts. It's getting to me. Lately, if no one else is around, he's gone to touching me."

Rivers was momentarily at a loss. "Groping, or something less than that?" he asked.

"Oh, mostly he'll just brush up against me. Yesterday he brushed my breast with his elbow—like it was an accident. And, it might have been, but I don't think so."

Rivers reflected on that. "Did anyone else see it?"

Willa said no, they had been in the concrete lab working a piece of equipment with two of the graduate students. The students left, and she and Haden were still going over part of the operating manual.

Suddenly Dr. Renfro seemed in a hurry to leave. She stood and started for the door, then stopped and turned back.

"Thanks for listening," she said. "Like I said, I don't want you to do anything. I just want to get my work done and get on with my career. My mid-probationary review is coming up. This is not the time to be having a big flap. And, in a couple of years, Haden will be voting on my tenure. Matt, I can't get crossways with these people."

Rivers was nonplussed. He knew he should do something, but he wasn't sure what. He stood there with his hands in his pockets, looking at her.

"Willa," he finally said, "let me think about this and get back to you."

He felt a little silly, but it was the best he could do at the moment. Dr. Renfro wanted him to know about Haden's behavior—alleged behavior, he reminded himself—but also wanted him to do nothing. He believed doing nothing was not an option, but what should be done was elusive. Haden, unknown to Renfro, had twice appealed his salary and threatened a grievance and maybe a lawsuit because his last attempt at promotion to full professor had been rebuffed. Jesse Small had provided this information on his way out the door. Rivers could envision John Haden claiming this whole thing was cooked up because of a bias against him.

After Willa Renfro left, Rivers stood staring out his office window for some while. Finally, he did the obvious thing. He called the dean. Actually, it would have been a better idea to reread the sexual harassment section of the university handbook and then call the dean, but it all worked out.

The dean's message was pretty straightforward, having been down this road before. Doing nothing was, indeed, not an option. Professor Renfro would just have to come to understand that. The fact that she was a valuable member of the department and that her career could be affected as well as Haden's had to be addressed effectively.

There was no reason to think the problem would go away and every reason to think it would get worse, leading to open conflict between the two people involved that would eventually spread who knew how far. From a pragmatic point of view, if it got worse and Haden did something really rash that could be proven, everyone would be liable and rightly so. In addition, this could be a matter of two ships passing in the night with totally different perceptions about the same set of facts. In any case, Haden had a right to know about the allegation.

The next step was to talk to someone in the affirmative action office. If the allegations were true and would meet the legal standard for sexual harassment, university policy demanded a formal investigation. If the allegations would fall short of that, a formal investigation might not be in order, but the matter could not be left there because the problem would just continue to fester. These things rarely, if ever, just went away.

The next day, Rivers met again with Dr. Renfro. He explained the department's obligation to address this problem and argued that, in the long term, it was in her best interest, too. She was very reluctant to proceed. In her view, she would be labeled a troublemaker. She just wanted Haden's behavior to stop.

In the end, Rivers and Renfro went together to share her concerns with an OAA officer. It became pretty evident that the legal standard might be met if the allegations could be proven, which would be difficult. Haden's alleged behavior seemed to be directed at her personally. Throughout the process, Dr. Renfro was pushing not to have a formal investigation. She never had such a thing in mind. She just wanted the whole thing to stop.

Ultimately, it was determined that the affirmative action officer and Rivers would review Professor Renfro's summary, which had been reduced to writing and signed by her, with Haden. They would get his side of the story, as well as his perceptions about it, and determine then if it warranted a formal investigation that would include most of the civil engineering faculty as witnesses.

When the two met with Haden, Anna Forbes, the affirmative action officer, did most of the talking. Haden was shocked—or at least did a convincing job of portraying shock. At one point, he broke down in tears. He claimed no memory of the breast-brushing incident. He did acknowledge telling a raunchy story or two, maybe more, in meetings, but had never directed them at Dr. Renfro or anyone else. At length, his statement was written up and signed by him.

At the end of the meeting, Forbes admonished Haden in no uncertain terms not to approach Dr. Renfro about this matter and not to do anything that could even remotely be considered as retaliation. He should not discuss this with others in the department. In the event of a formal investigation, they would be contacted. One or both of them would get back with him in a day or two.

As Haden was taking his leave, Anna Forbes asked him, "Dr. Haden, do you think Professor Renfro just made all this up?"

He paused a long time, his hand on the doorknob. "I can't imagine why she would," he said.

Rivers met with John Haden the next day. He explained that in lieu of a formal investigation, they would retain both his and Willa Renfro's statements in the affirmative action files and resolve the matter informally, if they could be assured that Haden would immediately cease any kind of offending behavior. Haden agreed to go out of his way to avoid any situation or action that could conceivably be construed as offensive. He took the extra step, eventually, of asking for a meeting with Dr. Renfro in Rivers' office. He apologized for anything he had done to offend her. She was agreeable to dropping the matter and accepted Haden's apology. Rivers made a note to his files, summarizing the content of the meeting. Things were a little tense at times for a few months, but eventually everyone put the incident behind them.

Why is this example of an affirmative action issue in a book about conflict resolution? Unfortunately, not all of theses situations turn out this well—either because they are allowed to go unaddressed until everyone has their heels dug in or because they are handled inappropriately. The adverse impact can damage careers needlessly and create schisms that last for years. Offending behavior such as this, intended or not, cannot be allowed. This case is treated here in some detail in order to make a number of points.

- Consider Rivers' position if he had not had the OAA to call on for assistance. He would be conducting a review of Dr. Renfro for tenure and promotion two years hence (assuming he was still chair). John Haden almost surely would be a candidate for promotion again. It was essential that he address this matter effectively in a way that would document fairness.

- If Anna Forbes had been an advocate for Willa Renfro, for example, in a hiring situation, she would have had a conflict of interest in this matter.

- Documentation was essential. However, it is much better to have such documentation in the OAA than in the departmental files.

- Rivers was a civil engineer, not someone trained in the nuances of employment law. He needed to access a higher level of expertise than he or the dean possessed.

- Haden had to be confronted with the situation. Fairness demanded that he know of the allegations about his behavior if they were not true, and, if they were, he needed to be aware of the potential consequences. If Rivers had done so alone, he could have been cast in the role of conducting a witch-hunt, something Haden could have used in a grievance if once again denied promotion. The involvement of a distant third party negated this.

- If Rivers had tried to resolve the matter by himself, on Renfro's behalf, he would have had the department in an uproar and been open to claims by her that he had dragged her into a confrontation against her will. Again, the involvement of a distant third party mitigates that possibility.

Some might argue that Professor Renfro should have confronted Dr. Haden herself. Some women would have. However, it is not easy for a probationary assistant professor to deal with someone who possesses some degree of influence over her future.

MULTICULTURAL AFFAIRS

Multicultural affairs can take on many names and faces, depending on the culture, organizational structure, and goals of the institution. By whatever name, this office (or person) becomes crucial to the process of DPRM in many ways. Regardless of title or configuration, the purpose of multicultural affairs is to further diversity throughout the institution. If not explicit in the beginning, it will—or should—become implicit that this includes gender as well as race. There are two primary components of this effort that apply to faculty and staff as well as to students: recruitment and retention. Central to both is the creation of an atmosphere conducive to the appreciation and utilization of the various strengths white men, women, and people of color bring to the advancement of the institution.

While this is part of everyone's job, the task is complicated and important enough to require specific leadership. The primary task of this person or office is to help lead the institution past politically correct rhetoric into real cultural change and sustainable programs. This is very difficult. It requires many skills that allow for a hard edge to push the envelope every day, a flexible side to build relationships and solve problems, and knowing when to ease off. The most important skill of all is that of broker.

Whether dealing with a dual career issue, women and at-risk faculty of color, climate problems in various departments, or disenfranchised students, people who specialize in this area must network with the chief academic officer, the deans, department heads and chairs, and specific key faculty. This networking must be used effectively to push the envelope on one hand and to solve problems (resolve conflict) on the other.

It is self-evident that people in the role of broker—to hire this person, mentor that one, buy time for another—cannot also be an adjudicator. One cannot be an advocate for a specific individual in one instance and impartially adjudicate that person's complaint in another.

People with these responsibilities catch many straws blowing in many winds. Thus, they have many opportunities to bring problems to the attention of people who might have the means to resolve them before they get out of hand. In order to seize these opportunities, these individuals must keep a water bucket under their desk, not a can of gasoline.

People who seek help in resolving problems through multicultural affairs often do not have a clear understanding of how the system works. It is essential that the leadership in multicultural affairs has this understanding and that its principals are well networked. This can be a key point for a multiple entry, multiple exit system of dispute resolution, that will be discussed in Chapter 8.

It also is the case that people acting in this capacity usually report to the chief academic officer. This creates an opportunity to convey concerns and obtain advice from that person, sometimes on behalf of anonymous third parties. If an individual with a problem, especially one involving race or gender, would like to know what the position, opinion, or advice of the provost might be in a given situation but is reluctant to approach her directly, someone in multicultural affairs can serve as an informal intermediary (as discussed in Chapter 7). This also gives the chief academic officer a heads up that something is in the wind so he can watch for an opportunity to pick up on it.

Some of these situations are generic and can provide a framework for addressing more widespread problems that can become a rich source of conflict. It is an important reality that people of color face more complications achieving tenure and promotion in predominantly white institutions. This is true for women as well, although increasing numbers may have begun to mitigate gender issues to some extent. To not recognize this is naïve. Some of the same dynamics apply to Asians and Asian Americans, but for the most part issues affecting them are different and are less inclined to get in the way of tenure and promotion.

Problems pertaining to promotion and tenure for women, African Americans, Hispanics, and other people, depending on their discipline, might include marginalization, difficulty finding collaborators and mentors, and differing views on what constitutes important research. Time devoted to serving as role models and mentors for students can drain away too much of their time, as can serving as a token presence on committees, especially search committees.

The leader of multicultural affairs should be a listening post for these kinds of concerns. She might arrange a luncheon for the tenure-track faculty of color, hosted by the chief academic officer, to get acquainted, check on their progress, and determine if they are finding needed support.

In one such real-life luncheon arranged for African American faculty by the associate provost for diversity and dual careers, I overheard the term *majority culture* used two or three times. At one point I asked, "Would someone describe the most important two or three characteristics that differentiate the majority culture (which meant white men) from the minority culture (which meant African Americans)?"

I expected a general response of some kind and a little give and take. I was wrong. Instead the response was succinct, articulate, and specific.

One of my colleagues responded, "The majority culture evaluates productivity on an individually competitive basis by counting and measuring things. The minority culture assesses individuals based on their contribution to furtherance of the (African American) community as a whole."

I never forgot those two lines. They changed my entire understanding of the issues in play for African Americans and Hispanics and, to some extent women, striving to succeed in academe.

The dichotomy of qualitative values in a quantitative system creates the certainty of conflict. Throughout the academy, promotion and tenure are based on counting and measuring things. There are valid reasons for placing importance on these things, but they take on a disproportionate impact because numbers lend themselves to objective assessment that is less demanding to evaluate and harder to challenge. But it works to the great disadvantage of people with a different value system and a different cultural starting point.

Dealing with this in terms of collective productivity, assurance of fairness, and management of conflict is everyone's responsibility. The leadership in multicultural affairs must play a key role in keeping all the moving parts of the effort headed in a positive direction.

ATTORNEYS

Lawyers are an important part of conflict management and dispute resolution in postsecondary institutions. All kinds of arrangements exist for the provision of legal service for the institution and its agents.

The larger the college or university, the more likely it is to have an internal legal staff. Virtually all doctoral granting research universities employ full-time legal counsel, usually amounting to a staff of several. Whatever the arrangement, several characteristics of the composite legal service are very important.

While there must be an understanding of the full spectrum of the law, most problems fall in the realm of employment law. However, large and important contract disputes do happen. For purposes of this discussion, employment law is fundamental.

Effective higher education lawyers must be adept at integrating the canon law (institutional policy, rules, regulations, and practices), politics, and fiscal realities with civil law. In colleges and universities, it is very rare for any one of these to operate alone.

An understanding must exist as to the balance of acting in good faith at the onset of a problem and protecting the legal interests of the institution. Openness and fairness can frequently lead to the early resolution of a potentially serious problem. This can involve some degree of risk as to the longer-term legal position of the college should the situation escalate. Striking a balance between these two interests is important for an effective working relationship among the institution, its administrators, and its lawyers.

As a dispute moves toward the likelihood of litigation, both the velvet glove and the steel fist must be accessible. College and university lawyers are important players in effective alternative dispute resolution and must understand how to further its successful application. However, not all cases can be settled internally or in the pretrial phase of litigation. When the institution and its agents are compelled to go to court, they must make every effort to win. The institution should only go to court in cases that are 1) very important, and 2) possible, even likely, to be won. Losing in court is in no one's interest. The institution will appear to have been at fault and potential plaintiffs against it will feel encouraged. Those rare individuals who delight in keeping the institution stirred up will be empowered, to the detriment of the working environment. None of these results of losing in court help future efforts aimed at alternative dispute resolution.

The lawyer's role must be clear to all the parties. An institution's lawyer has only one client—the institution. When individual legal interests diverge from those of the institution, the individual must retain his own counsel. Who pays the legal fees in such circumstances must be clear in advance, most likely through policy.

7 ◆ KEY COLLATERAL PLAYERS: SUPPORT AND SPECIALITY PERSONNEL

In thinking through an institutional approach to the prevention, resolution, and management of conflict, it is easy to overlook a category of very important people. These players in the conflict and dispute arena might be faculty, administrators, or staff. Sometimes they are outsiders, depending on the circumstances. They are characterized here under the labels of trusted intermediaries, counselors and coaches, and staff. While their seemingly disparate roles are less sharply defined than those in Chapters 5 and 6, they are very important.

TRUSTED INTERMEDIARIES

Some people have a knack for solving problems, especially those directly related to people and personalities. They have several characteristics in common. Prominent among these is that people trust them because they are honest, discreet, and not inclined to gossip. They treat everyone well, regardless of station. People rarely are appointed to such a role; they acquire it over time.

Trusted intermediaries may be faculty in an academic department, staff (especially secretarial staff, to whom we will return), or general administrators. They are knowledgeable about how the institution operates and have a sense of who to talk to about various situations. If appointed to a position of ombudsperson, these people would be extraordinarily effective, but they are more valuable in their informal role, partly because they do not acquire baggage at the same rate as an ombudsman.

It goes without saying that *opposites* of these people also exist, thankfully in smaller number. The *opposites* pick up word of a problem and infuse it into the gossip mill. They leap to conclusions and spread them like the truth. There is no discernible difference between fact and opinion for the *opposites*. They cannot be trusted to help solve problems but can be depended upon to create them if someone with an axe to grind provides an opportunity. If a fire breaks out, the *opposites* always have a can of gasoline handy to throw on it. They then bask in its light.

The term *trusted intermediaries* begs the question, "Trusted by whom?" The answer: by disputing parties and by people in positions of responsibility who are accountable for ensuring that disputes and unproductive conflicts are resolved fairly and effectively. As a side effect, trusted intermediaries tend to cast a positive influence on interpersonal disputes and bring reason to departmental conflict and to disputes between faculty governance and administration. When a fire breaks out they throw water on it. The following situation is an example of how such people can be a very positive influence.

Emma Staley was black; a first generation woman who came up through a Historically Black University. She arrived at North State University ABD (all but dissertation). When she finished her degree, the journalism school wanted to hire her, and she wanted to stay. A position opened at the right time, and the university made a direct appointment. Now she was nearing the end of the second year of a tenure-track appointment as an assistant professor.

A few days earlier, Emma had arranged to stop by for a visit with Chet Alexander. Chet was a full professor in the English department who was considering a job in administration. The opportunity had presented itself when the provost had conducted a short internal search for acting associate provost for academic affairs. Chet, white male though he was, had been a slam-dunk.

Just about everyone wanted him. His leadership as chair of a major university-wide task force on future priorities a couple of years before had consolidated a generally positive feeling about him and his ability. His area of specialty was ethnic linguistics, and this brought him in contact with a lot of undergraduate students of color.

Chet Alexander got Emma Staley and himself situated around the little conference table in the corner of his office. He had yet to take naturally to wearing a tie to work, so some days he didn't. This was a no-tie day, mitigated to some degree by an elegant mock turtleneck sweater and new sport coat. He settled into his chair across from Emma, one hand on the tabletop and one on the arm of his chair. He glanced out the window (a big step up from his faculty office under the eaves of Frazier Hall) and then looked at Emma.

"What's up?" he asked.

Emma was obviously a little uneasy. "I don't know if I have a problem or not," she said, "and if I do, I certainly am not sure what to do about it."

Alexander waited for more, but there was a pause. Emma was an elegant woman with an engaging manner. In his opinion, she had done North State a lot of good. The faculty was just about all white, but the number of black and Hispanic students was increasing and they needed someone to look up to and to be a mentor. He knew from his experience with student groups that they trusted Emma, and a few of them had come to depend on her.

Chet had a little ceramic polar bear on the table top, something one of his daughters had given him for a birthday present a couple of years before. Emma was pushing it back and forth between her thumb and forefinger. "A gift from our youngest daughter," he offered. "She was five at the time."

"Cute," Emma replied. She paused, obviously in deep thought, and went on. "I am not making the kind of progress I need to in my research," she said. "I have some things underway,

but beyond getting some contacts made in a number of newspapers and setting up a process for gathering data, I haven't gotten much of a start."

Alexander already knew her research was in racial bias in print media. *"How is the teaching going?"* he inquired.

"Really well." Alexander already knew this because he had heard as much from numerous students. *"And, I love it. The students really seem to respond to me."*

"So, why the concern?"

Emma explained that Jack Snell, the director of the School of Journalism, had just done her annual review for reappointment. The faculty input was to the effect that although Emma's teaching was very good, the school was trying to expand its research. Several thought her progress was not sufficient at this point for her to get tenure when the time came unless she took it up a notch, maybe two notches in her research. In meeting with her the previous week, Snell had said that he tended to agree with that assessment. He had been less explicit in his letter to her than in their private meeting.

"I have a problem that is very common among black people in academe," Emma went on. *"I love teaching and I am very good at it. I really enjoy research, although my approach doesn't quite jibe with what a couple of the older print faculty think is important."*

Emma picked up the little polar bear and held it in her hand, her long black fingers cradling it gently.

"The underlying problem is that I tie up a lot of time with students, especially black students, and most of all those who are struggling. The majority of them are first generation, just like me. How can I not give them my time? But then I lack the time to keep my research moving."

Alexander knew this to be true. He also knew that some of these students would drop out if they did not have a mentor and role model that could coach them through the rough spots. *"Isn't this something you should be able to work out with Jack Snell?"*

he asked. "Or if not him, then the dean." By this he meant the dean of arts and sciences, in whose college the journalism school resided.

Emma placed the bear in the center of the table. "Jack says that he knows the student work is important, but I can never make tenure without an active research program and some real productivity in terms of publications. I know four or five of the senior faculty have talked to him about that and basically put pressure on him not to make any exceptions. Unfortunately, I don't know about the dean. He and Jack go back a long way. They are close friends. I have met him only socially a time or two."

"Speaking of other faculty," Chet replied, "how do you get on with the rest of the department?"

Emma allowed as how everyone was cordial and now and again she was invited to lunch by one or more of her colleagues. A couple of times she had collaborated with one of them on a student project and had been asked to give several guest lectures. But when it came to her research, there was no collaboration. In part, she reckoned, that was due to the subject matter, as no one else had a primary interest in it.

This was yet another new experience for Chet Alexander. He wasn't sure what he should do, if anything. "Let me visit with the provost about this," he said.

Emma was nervous about that. "I don't want him to get involved," she said. "I don't want anything done, especially, I just needed to talk to someone and figure out what to do."

"Nothing formal. I would just like to bounce it off him. Sometimes he has some good insight into how to deal with these situations in a subtle way."

"Just don't let it look to the dean or to Jack like I went around them to complain to the provost," Emma said.

"Well," Chet responded after a moment of reflection, "you didn't, did you? You talked to me about something that concerned you. You certainly have not lodged a complaint of any kind."

Chet Alexander did discuss the matter with the provost during their weekly session to gather loose ends. He was careful to explain that Emma Staley was not lodging a complaint. She just needed some good advice. The provost felt that such advice should come from her dean, not from him.

That made sense to Alexander. "But," he asked, "how do we get that to happen?"

While not exactly old hat, this kind of situation was not new to the provost. "How about you finding the right moment to tell the dean that you happened to be visiting with Emma Staley and you got the impression something was bothering her. You could go on to suggest that since she is a young assistant professor and one of only two African Americans in his whole college, it might be a good idea if he asked her in for a visit, just to see how she is getting along."

By "find the right moment," Chet Alexander knew the provost did not mean to write the man a letter, or even to call him up about this specific matter. A couple of days later, he met the dean on the sidewalk outside of the student union. After an exchange of pleasantries (he was, after all, Chet's dean also), Chet said, "I happened to be visiting with Emma Staley a few days ago. She really is a sharp lady. I run into her a lot with my student linguistics projects. Anyway, I got the impression something was bothering her. What would you think about inviting her over for a visit, and see if you think she is progressing all right?"

The dean was not just hatched the evening before. He immediately knew without going into detail that this represented an opportunity to prevent a serious problem instead of doing damage control two or three years hence.

"Thanks for bringing that up," he replied. "I should have done it already. I will have Emma over for a visit and get an update on her progress."

Of course, the dean learned all the same things that Chet already knew, but he was in a position to make adjustments. Furthermore, he did so through a little hands-on mentoring of both Emma Staley and Jack Snell.

There are some important points to be gleaned from this scenario. Emma Staley knew she had a problem and was willing to take the initiative in getting it on the table. Chet Alexander showed good listening skills and more than a little common sense. His goal was to contribute to solving a problem before it escalated. He also understood the art of subtle diplomacy. An *opposite* would have put his own ego out front and done something precipitous, like writing an anonymous letter to the affirmative action office alerting them to an injustice going on in the School of Journalism. The provost had chosen wisely in hiring Alexander in the first place. The same for hiring the dean. He trusted them to act responsibly and to let him know if they hit a snag. The dean comes in for special consideration. He could have gotten defensive. Sensing that Emma Staley probably had sought out Chet Alexander, he was smart enough and understanding enough to realize why that might have happened and to seize the opportunity to save himself and, most of all, Emma, a lot of unnecessary grief.

This example case could have been handled a lot of different ways. Unfortunately, most of them lead to angry memos and emails, formal complaints and estrangement. It should be noted that Chet Alexander was a university insider, so to speak. He had proven himself to be a right-minded problem solver, not a confrontational egocentric. Every institution must bring new blood into the administration from time to time. However, this should not be done just for the sake of "going outside." When a new person does come into an institution, she should be sensitive to the realities of the unique culture and expectations as to how things get done. Sometimes these may need to be changed, but not immediately. Insiders with an understanding of these things, and of individual people, are invaluable *if* their motives are positive and they have good people skills. Deployment of *opposites* in such roles at any time, especially by a person new to the institution, is sure to precipitate large problems.

In a way, Chet Alexander also acted as a counselor or a coach. But for purposes of creating a systemic approach to conflict management, those terms apply to another kind of individual.

COUNSELOR AND COACH

One might think of a counselor or a coach as a mentor and, in a sense, they can be. But we are after something different here. An institution and its people can derive great benefit from what one might think of as human systems expertise. People possessing these skills can come from a variety of experiences and educational backgrounds, but they are professionals certified in a related field. This is what sets them apart from trusted intermediaries.

Such professionals have expertise in resolution of conflict between individuals and within and between groups. They can act as facilitators and as diagnosticians. They can function as an executive coach, for lack of a better term. Most institutions have individuals within them who have these skills. The most common location for these services is in human resources or its equivalent, if they are located within the institution.

A human systems consultant, or internal employee for that matter, can provide a number of essential services to the institution *if* he understands how it works. Some individuals can do this and some cannot. Having the basic skill set is not enough. The person must also be able to identify the nature of the institution.

Individuals, or the person to whom they report, often need help to resolve a dispute or ongoing conflict. Sometimes the chemistry between two individuals just does not work. Most people want to resolve issues and go forward. A few do not. A professional with the right skills and experience can often guide those that do through a reconciliation process. In other instances, the person to whom an individual reports, for example, a department chair, can be coached about how to take the role of facilitator most effectively.

Academics who get into administration usually do so on the strength of their academic accomplishment and indication of interest. Many of these individuals have a lot to offer and just need some experience, training, and mentoring. Some have a flaw that will impede their progress or cause them to fail. This is unfortunate for the individual and causes problems for the institution, including the loss of considerable talent. Of course, the best time to avoid this situation is in hiring.

However, when corrective measures are needed, it is unwise to start by throwing the baby out with the bath water. One of the most common problems is temper. Another is the inability to address issues in a timely and candid manner face-to-face. A good human systems consultant, outside the hierarchy and with the right know-how, can coach some individuals through these shortcomings.

It is not uncommon for personality-driven group dynamics to get in the way of the productive functioning of a unit, such as an academic department. A department head or chair, working elbow to elbow with individuals in the group, may find it very difficult to get the department on track. A completely independent outsider with no axe to grind and no power within the institution can be very helpful, for example, in facilitating a strategic planning process. Someone who has professional-level skills in assessing and guiding group dynamics can be much more valuable in such a situation than another outsider in the same academic discipline as the disputants.

Some of the most vexing problems develop around individuals who exhibit particular patterns of behavior. In some instances, such people feel damaged by the institution; in others, they seem to thrive on conflict. The section on trusted intermediaries referred to such individuals as *opposites*. They love to bask in the reflected light of fires they start or accelerate. Preventing their activities from disrupting entire sectors of the institution while attempting to recoup their positive participation can be a real challenge. Professional help can be a necessity for those responsible for getting such individuals back on track. A good human systems consultant can help diagnose the dynamics of the situation and provide real assistance to the parties responsible for developing a corrective strategy.

If a person with human systems expertise is not presently employed, the institutional impulse may be to rush out and hire one. This impulse should be resisted until the following important issues have been thought through.

People experiencing the kind of problems described earlier are often reluctant to go to internal employees for help, understandably so. They worry that their problem will become part of the grapevine, that they will be regarded as a troublemaker, or that distorted versions of the situation will reach people who will hold sway over their careers. Free and unfettered access to highly qualified help without needing to get signed vouchers for payment or wading through the bureaucracy to get an appointment can be an incentive to seek assistance in finding real solutions.

Also, people who are hired as full-time, regular employees can be very hard to dismiss if they don't work out. They take on a role in the institution and expand the administrative bureaucracy in ways that tend to permanence. Outsiders hired on contract are subject to discontinuance. If a human systems consultant is not working out, it is easy to terminate one arrangement and establish another. If budget reductions are necessary, the size of the retainer can be reduced.

Over time, employees working in personnel situations risk accumulating baggage. They are part of a community, talking with other employees in both professional and social situations. They develop relationships with some people and not others. Their perspectives can become slanted or can be perceived as such. Once this happens, a person's effectiveness in the role of counselor or coach is compromised.

Outsiders have no authority in the institution and no ties to anyone who does. People can use the services of such an individual without fear that the matter at hand will become part of the common wisdom or come back to haunt them in the evaluation and reward process.

Creation of a structured arrangement whereby the institution can be well served with human systems expertise within the framework of its culture and canon law can be implemented through a contractual arrangement with an outside professional. Candidates can be screened and a selection made based on criteria established by the institution and its agents. A key element of the relationship is that it be done on a retainer basis with an hourly fee that allows employees to seek these services on a strictly work-related basis without getting permission or signing vouchers. Confidentiality must be assured, with the exception that a senior administrator, such as the chief academic officer, be informed of situations which affect the welfare of the institution, but only with the user's knowledge.

STAFF

An administrator who might benefit from a human systems consultant will derive even more support from outstanding staff.

In his book *Academic Leadership,* Leaming (1998) frames the first chapter around a list of best practices. One of these is "Hire a Good Secretary." Bull's eye.

It is absolutely essential to hire and retain excellent staff in order to prevent conflict. The impact on the effectiveness of the administrator to whom the person reports, or the host of faculty and other staff she encounters over time, is all too easy to underestimate. Whether these people have titles such as administrative assistant, secretary, accountant, or something else, they must be effective at the core job requirement *and* possess good people skills. The more out front they are, the more essential the people skills.

A secretary or administrative assistant in a business office, whether it is that of department head, dean, or provost, has a lot of work to do and talks to a lot of people. He (although it usually is she) creates the first impression people have of the office and the relevant administrator. Angry people, be they parents, students, faculty, or other staff, tend to vent their spleen on such individuals, then be respectful and even ingratiating to their boss. When one spends the day on the telephone, processing words, keeping track of department accounts, and answering innumerable questions about where to go for what, and then serves as the first point of encounter with people bearing complaints, reality about one's compatibility with this line of work sets in quickly. Unfortunately, people in these roles are almost always underpaid. It is not enough for these individuals to be industrious and do high-quality work. They absolutely must be good with people. Central to this aspect of the job is the ability to keep their cool, treat everyone with respect, and solve problems within the limits of their job description. I have been blessed with people like this. They made me more effective and had a positive impact on the institution.

Information technology (IT) staff fall into this same category but in a very different way. Historically, IT work happened in a comparatively closed environment. Now, it permeates the institution. It takes an extremely focused skill set and intense concentration. Those skills do not always come with a gregarious nature. Until recently, this was not much of an issue. However, over the past 10 years, as institutions have integrated IT into the very fabric of their work, people in these specialties must offer the same high level of expertise in their field as well as a strong service ethic and ability to work as part of a team that permeates all aspects of the institution.

This is very difficult. I could not begin to do what many of these people accomplish as a matter of course, nor could I ever learn it. I cannot count the times their dedicated efforts have saved my institution from collapse, especially as security has become a big issue. They are often under enormous pressure. Working straight through a weekend is common when a new worm bursts over the horizon and threatens to shut down an institution. Add to this milieu several hundred or thousand faculty and administrators, all with highly individualized needs and quirky schedules, who need help *now,* and the challenges escalate. Conflict can burst forth in all its manifestations. People are not trained to manage this. They learn it over time. The right organizational structure (individualized to each institution) and large doses of professional development opportunity are essential features for evolving successfully in the face of the incredible, relentless change that characterizes this field. Professional development in this field today must include people issues as well as technological challenges.

Every pressure point in the institution experiences the same phenomena at some level. In research universities, another good example of a make-or-break impact of the staff is the office that processes the final version of all grant and contract proposals and gets them out the door. If highly motivated faculty come in on the last day before a deadline and need help finalizing the budget and obtaining all the requisite signatures but encounter a grouchy staff member who starts by listing all the reasons why this cannot possibly happen, careers are affected and conflict is sparked. If this is the general attitude in the office, the chief research officer will spend much time putting out brush fires instead of bringing people together to develop exciting new ideas. On the other hand, if investigators encounter a pleasant, can-do attitude and an effective grant and contract office, they are going to feel better about getting their next proposal moving. Usually, squeaking past deadlines in a research office requires extra effort on the part of the staff. It is not uncommon for them to push through evenings and weekends, especially when federal agency deadlines are clustered in time. The good ones do it and take pride in doing it well. And it helps immensely when they get a sincere expression of appreciation from their clients.

The list of examples could go on. These are obvious ones that make the point. The staff members that serve in innumerable positions of support comprise a personality-rich infrastructure that makes the institution function. Academic institutions have one thing to sell—the talent of the faculty. Everything else is in support of that. However, that support must be effective, both in getting the work done and in contributing to a culture and environment that are conducive to maximizing the intellectual energy that the academic enterprise is all about.

Staff-supported activities can provide a rich opportunity to move the institution forward. On the other hand, they can drag it down through dissent and the rumor mill. Careful cultivation of a positive climate in this arena is a key component of preventing unproductive conflict.

8 ◆ Putting It All Together: Creating an Integrated System of Dispute Prevention, Resolution, and Management

Identifying the Component Parts

The fact that conflict and disputes can be addressed effectively through formal and informal means does not speak against a structured, integrated system. Rather, it calls for the realization that informal approaches to addressing disputes should be viewed as part of a total system. A workable schema of dispute resolution must have several characteristics.

- It must be based on clear, easily accessible policy.

- It must include a statement of the core values of the institution.

- It must have a complete set of compatible moving parts.

- The people involved in its operation must know each other personally, understand each other's role, and trust each other.

- It must have multiple entry and multiple exit points.

- Overall responsibility for its implementation must reside with a specific individual.

- It must be accompanied by ongoing education and professional development to ensure sustainability.

Each of these components will be discussed in the context of a complete working system, recognizing that all have been addressed in a different (free-standing) context heretofore.

POLICY

A complete description of the system must be widely available. Brochures work well for this, but a user-friendly web site is a must. The, big advantage of a web site is convenience of access at all hours as well as the ease with which it can be revised. A web site lends itself to easy distribution to all administrators, faculty, and staff, including new employees as part of the orientation process.

A summation of relevant policy per se is not limited to policy about dispute resolution specifically. All conflict has seeds that germinated somewhere, and the most prolific breeding grounds can be identified. The most common include:

- Promotion and tenure policy and guidelines

- Policy and guidelines for annual performance evaluation

- Policy and procedures for addressing discrimination and harassment complaints related to race and gender

- Appeal and grievance policy

- Standards and procedures for nonreappointment of faculty and staff

- Review and reappointment/nonreappointment of administrators

- Faculty policy on academic integrity

- Criteria, standards, and procedures for dismissal of tenured faculty

- Policy and procedures for provision of ombudspersons

- Policy and procedures for provision of mediation services

- Consulting policy

- Policy governing ownership of intellectual property

This list will vary in length and content by institution, depending on the local construct of policy, procedure, practice, and custom. The essential point is that all policies, procedures, and customs designed to address conflict or controversial circumstances comprise a body of work integral to dispute prevention, resolution, and management (DPRM). The various relevant policies must comprise a coherent whole and be clearly stated and readily accessible. All the players in Chapters 5, 6, and 7 must be thoroughly familiar with the policies or comfortable with locating and interpreting them.

STATEMENT OF CORE VALUES

I am indebted to my colleagues in the shared governance of Kansas State University, and to Dr. Cia Verschelden in particular, for their assertion of the concept that a university should have a clear written statement as to the core values by which it lives. This means core values with regard to people, not programs. They were right. Since May 2001, Kansas State University has had such a statement posted in every work area and classroom in the university. It is reproduced here as an example.

KANSAS STATE UNIVERSITY
PRINCIPLES OF COMMUNITY

Kansas State University is a land-grant, public research university, committed to teaching and learning, research, and service to the people of Kansas, the nation, and the world. Our collective mission is best accomplished when every member of the university community acknowledges and practices the following principles:

- We affirm the inherent dignity and value of every person and strive to maintain an atmosphere of justice based on respect for each other.

- We affirm the right of each person to freely express thoughts and opinions in a spirit of civility and decency. We believe that diversity of views enriches our learning environment and we promote open expression within a climate of courtesy, sensitivity, and mutual respect.

- We affirm the value of human diversity for community. We confront and reject all forms of prejudice and discrimination, including those based on race, ethnicity, gender, age, disability, sexual orientation, religious or political beliefs, economic status, or any other differences that have led to misunderstanding, hostility, and injustice.

- We acknowledge that we are a part of the larger Kansas community and that we have an obligation to be engaged in a positive way with our civic partners.

- We recognize our individual obligations to the university community and to the principles that sustain it. We will each strive to contribute to a positive spirit that affirms learning and growth for all members of the community.

The president, provost, and dean of the graduate school signed the statement for the university. The president of the graduate council, president of the faculty senate, president of student government, president of the graduate student council, and president of classified senate, signed as they were constituted in May 2001. The statement has had a positive effect on the working atmosphere. That is not to say it is a panacea. However, it creates a comprehensive frame of reference in which to address conflict, especially that which stems from bad behavior.

A Set of Compatible Moving Parts

The body of policy, procedure, practice, and custom, along with a statement of institutional core values, comprise the fixed parts of the system. The people that make the system work comprise the moving parts. This list of parts will vary and the individual duties will be modified according to institutional characteristics, culture, and structure. However, to recap briefly from Chapters 5, 6, and 7, the following officers and offices play key roles, whatever their title, at a given institution.

- *The governing board.* The role of the board will vary over a broad range, depending on the nature of the institution. In many instances, the board may never be directly involved in specific disputes, but in every instance it has overall responsibility for ensuring that appropriate policies and procedures are in place and that executive performance in this area is effective.

- *The president or chancellor.* The chief executive officer has overall responsibility for ensuring that the appropriate officer(s) is maintaining effective policy and procedures and performing effectively, hands-on, in conflict situations. The president/chancellor also plays a critical role in creating and maintaining an atmosphere of trust and mutual respect.

- *The provost or vice president for academic affairs.* In most instances, the chief academic officer will be the individual charged with specific responsibility for oversight of an effective system of DPRM, at least in academic affairs. Depending on the size, culture, and organizational structure of the institution, this responsibility will be carried out in collaboration with other vice presidents. In terms of ensuring an effective system within the academic community, however, this officer is the one that the president should hold accountable for a workable program.

- *The academic deans.* While not directly part of the institution-wide system, the deans must know how to work with it in addressing conflict in their areas of responsibility. This relationship and the resources within the system become key elements in their efforts. The deans play especially critical roles in adapting an institution-wide, integrated system to the culture and aims of their college.

- *Department heads and chairs and other unit leaders.* Day in and day out, these individuals work at the frontlines of DPRM. They must have the basic skills upon which to build, and they will benefit in significant ways from additional training. When trouble breaks out, they must have effective help, the first line of assistance being their dean as well as specific resources in the institution-wide system.

- *Ombudspersons.* While the Office of the Ombudsman may be an inclusive problem-solving resource at some institutions, the point here is to include the need for impartial assistance to employees in getting their concerns articulated properly and addressed effectively through appropriate channels, be they formal or informal.

- *Mediators.* Mediation can be handled by independent mediators external to the institution or by employees with proper training. Mediation is a necessary part of a complete system of conflict prevention, resolution, and management, and must be conducted by properly qualified individuals.

- *The Office of Affirmative Action.* By whatever name, the entity within the institution that deals proactively with race, gender, age, national origin, sexual orientation, disability, and veteran status plays a key role in an effective system of DPRM. It is the first point of contact for many, especially women and people of color, even if the primary issue is not race or gender related. It must be able to function as an open door to other aspects of the system, as well as continue to serve its primary purpose.

- *The Office of Multicultural Affairs.* This person or office encounters innumerable disputes and areas of conflict. Frequently, these are in the early stages and are subject to successful intervention. This person or office also has a unique feel for the campus climate of diversity-related issues.

- *The university attorney(s).* The institution may have full-time attorneys as employees, or it may serve these needs through one or more private individuals on a part-time or contract basis. In either event, the attorney(s) serving the legal interests of the institution must view himself as part of a broader system of DPRM and understand his role in matters of both civil and canon law within this context. If this is not the case, it is natural for an attorney to move too quickly and too aggressively to protect the legal interests of the institution in ways that impede informal resolution of disputes.

- *The union or bargaining unit.* While not addressed in depth in this book, if a union or bargaining unit is present on campus, its role must be clear with reference to conflict and disputes. The relevant policy will, in all likelihood, be part of the bargaining process and, in some instances, the union has responsibility for grievances.

- *Trusted intermediaries.* Trusted intermediaries come in many shapes and sizes and may be situated in any number of positions. They must be widely trusted, discrete, and endowed with an eminent level of common sense. Their radar must be on at all times. If they meet these qualifications, they can be of remarkable value to the smooth functioning of the institution.

115

- *Counselor and coach.* When department heads and chairs and deans have free access to expertise in human systems they will develop a sense of when to seek this kind of help. It should be emphasized here that this person is best situated outside the institution, working as an independent contractor in contact with the chief academic officer, and on a retainer to eliminate the impediment of university officers having to seek permission for engagement of her services.

- *Staff.* The term *staff* means every support person who serves one of the just mentioned offices or officers. Specific personnel serving in these roles often have the first encounter with people who are affected by emotions ranging from fear to anger. It is essential that they receive courteous and competent attention from staff at this first point of contact.

KNOWING AND TRUSTING EACH OTHER

This may be the most important point of all. It is essential that the moving institution-wide parts (the players involved in the process) know each other personally. Department heads and chairs and deans and their associates and assistants can be engaged through a separate professional development effort. This means each individual must understand what each of the others does and, to some extent, how they do it. They must have a sense of the individual personalities as well as the collective personality of the group.

A good, up-to-date web site will be helpful to individuals who play a direct role in conflict management and dispute resolution. Newsletters can also contribute to the information component, but this quickly can become a form of overkill and people tend not to read them. However, neither of these approaches to disseminating information addresses the hands on, personal aspect.

One very effective way to personally communicate information is to have a luncheon meeting of the entire group at least twice a year. The luncheon period allows people to get acquainted or reacquainted on an informal basis. The meeting afterward allows each person to re-introduce herself, explain what she does, and review any issue that is impacting her area of work.

It is very important for such a get together to be hosted by the person with overall responsibility for establishment and maintenance of this system. Normally this would be the chief academic officer. Although this person should delegate many duties, this is not one of them. The responsible officer must attend the event, lead the activity, and take a knowledgeable role in the discussion in order to reinforce the importance of the effort. This also is the only sure way to get a feel for how the system is working and what kind of adjustments need to be made.

MULTIPLE POINTS OF ENTRY AND EXIT

An essential feature of a workable, user-friendly system is that people with issues can enter it in any one or more of a number of points in a flexible manner. The same is true for moving from one avenue of resolution to another.

The most common point of entry is the ombudsperson, although department heads and chairs and affirmative action officers also rank high. It would not be unusual for a dean or chief academic officer to refer disputing parties to a facilitator or mediator as part of an appeal process. It is very common for an affirmative action officer, upon determining that a specific complaint does not rise to the legal standard of discrimination, to direct the complainant into another avenue of dispute resolution.

People who are frustrated with their circumstances, overwhelmed by a convergence of problems, timid by nature, or new to the institution often have difficulty taking the first step in getting their issue articulated to someone who can do something about it. It is essential that information about pathways to problem solving in general and dispute resolution in particular be readily available. Pamphlets can help, and a good, user-friendly web site can help more. Most importantly, the number of people who have some sense of how the system works must be large enough that concerned people are likely to find help just by talking to an acquaintance or colleague. When they go see an ombudsperson, their department head, or an affirmative action officer, that person must be knowledgeable about the various avenues available. If the first contact does not yield a tangible outcome, it must, at a minimum, provide direction to one that will.

In short, there can be no dead ends. Some worry that when more avenues are created for problem resolution, more problems will occur. This has not been the case in my experience. People generally have a positive outlook and want to be successful (although I would be quick to acknowledge that this is by no means universal). The real issue is that when attempts to resolve conflict meet with dead ends, instances of smoldering anger and frustration accumulate among the faculty and staff. These lead to brushfires. Sometimes these brushfires converge into a real inferno. At a minimum, they drag down the intellectual vibrancy of the institution.

OVERALL RESPONSIBILITY WITH A SPECIFIC INDIVIDUAL

Fragmentation of conflict management efforts will ensure a low-quality program and a lot of dead-end attempts at dispute resolution. Division of responsibility between executive officers can augment this. Although each segment of the university might have its own system, such an approach would be very inefficient. However, each major unit does have unique characteristics. For example, the vice president for administration and facilities (by whatever name) has overall responsibility for a large number of clerical staff, accountants, and so forth, but also for custodians and skilled craftsmen. The culture and many of the issues encountered in this area are significantly different than those arising among the faculty and academic support staff.

The chief academic officer also has responsibility for a substantial number of clerical staff, computing and technology specialists, and unclassified professional staff of several sorts. The primary difference is the faculty and the attendant arcane system of tradition and custom that accompanies them and their work. Two factors loom large in this milieu: tenure and the various cultures that attend each discipline. As a rule, faculty members are much more outspoken than others and play a much larger role in governance of the institution. A large body of policy exists that governs their role and that of the administration.

As a practical matter, a core of dispute resolution services is needed to serve the entire university with specific variations that address local unique needs. It makes the most sense for the chief academic officer to have overall responsibility for this core of institution-wide services because the most complex and diverse activities are in academic affairs. However, the areas of commonality and difference must be understood, and the executive officers must be collaborative and generally conversant about how the system works and how collectively they can constantly improve it.

EDUCATION AND PROFESSIONAL DEVELOPMENT

The most potentially effective system of conflict management in the world will do no good if no one knows about it. For effective engagement to develop, there must be a critical mass of collective understanding across the institution about the various pathways for dispute resolution and how they work and interact.

Information must be easily and widely available to faculty and staff. Those situated at the points where conflict most commonly surfaces must be well informed about the system and confident in it. These would include department heads and chairs, faculty leaders (and union officials if they exist in the institution), affirmative action officers, multicultural affairs, the women's center (under whatever name), and so forth. Most important of all may be the ombudspersons. An especially important point of education is at the annual new faculty (and staff) orientation, in whatever form it takes. While such an item might not fit into a new faculty ice cream social, it fits right into the survival kit session.

Once all these people in the institution are educated about the system and how it works, one can breathe a sigh of relief—right? Wrong!

119

People come and go in any work environment, and academe is no different. Over a 10-year period, most of the deans and department heads as well as the executive officers will have changed. The faculty leadership is elected anew every year. Ombudspersons may have specific terms, usually short. Full-time, long-term ombudspersons accumulate baggage; some can continue to be effective, some cannot. An ongoing education process aimed at these categories of university personnel is absolutely essential. It must be part of both the policy and practice of the institution. The chief academic officer must be clearly responsible for making it happen, at least in academic affairs, and be held accountable for it by the president. Without this, the system will fall into disarray within two or three years.

Before leaving this discussion about developing an effective system of DPRM, it should be emphasized again that the system creates an architecture within which the majority of problems get solved early and informally. The essential nature of immediate, informal conflict management and dispute resolution cannot be overemphasized. However, all too many disputes escape early, informal intervention, so there must be a systematic, integrated means of addressing them before they get out of hand.

9 ◆ SOME BEST PRACTICES

FACT-FINDING AND BASIC FAIRNESS

Conflict management and dispute resolution can happen consistently only when predicated on trust. Trust is predicated on basic fairness. Fairness can only be established on truth. Truth can only be established on facts, insofar as they can be known. Thus, everyone who plays a role in dispute resolution must be inculcated in the idea that fact-finding is central and that no position is to be taken in any adjudication process, formal or informal, until the facts have been established. This is the only way to make fairness as certain as possible.

There is another aspect of fairness—fairness to whom? When I was appointed as provost of Kansas State University, my wife gave me one piece of advice on the first day: Be fair. That is summative wisdom at its best. Indeed, I had every intention of being fair and have worked to do so ever since, although not with universal success. One of the central complications was to whom I was obligated to be fair. The easy answer is the person making a complaint or being complained against. It is all too easy to get caught up in thinking only about fairness to the individual at the center of the issue. However, the right answer is everyone who is a legitimate stakeholder in the issue under consideration. At an academic institution, this usually includes colleagues in the complainant's unit, students, tuition payers, and taxpayers.

One can quickly see how commitment to thoroughness in fact-finding and identification of the stakeholders in a conflict are fundamental to basic fairness, along with establishing the principles or interests the parties wish to serve.

PRACTICE INTEREST-BASED NEGOTIATION

Every party to a dispute has one or more interests they want to serve. Sometimes these coincide, but usually not. Identifying these interests is key, whether the process is formal or informal. Of course, this is the very basis of mediation, but it also is critical to informal efforts to resolve disputes. These interests are not always immediately evident. The stated complaint might, for example, be that the person's department chair marginalizes her, and as a result her productivity is not where she would like it. Her salary has suffered as a consequence. It might then come to light that in one specific incident, the chair made an especially disparaging remark to her in a faculty meeting that she found hurtful and embarrassing. In an instance like this, a key interest might be a sincere apology. This would have more value if it were made in another faculty meeting.

Sometimes issues of personal pride are key interests, especially when others offstage who are close to the complainant are pressuring them in some way. For example, an associate professor who is denied promotion to full professor might be willing to wait another year and accomplish some key element of work were it not for pressure from a spouse. This kind of issue is not likely to be stated by the parties, but putting oneself in the disputants' shoes can help a great deal in determining the interests of individuals or groups, or at least in interpreting what they consider them to be.

APPLY THE REASONABLE PERSON TEST

The outcome of any effort to resolve a dispute must be satisfactory to the parties. But in the fiduciary fishbowl of postsecondary education, especially public higher education, the outcome must withstand scrutiny from regents, administrators, faculty (leaders), legislators and their staff, auditors, special interest groups, the spouses and friends of all these people, and so forth. In general, the public and their representatives understand the idea of basic fairness. Even though reasonable people disagree about many things, they tend to evaluate the factors in a situation and make reasonable assessments about the internal logic of the outcome. This is important, even though it may be done in hindsight.

So who is this reasonable person? She is everyman. To gain a perspective of the reasonable person's view, put yourself in the position of each of the parties and all of the stakeholder categories. Seek the opinion and perspective of others (within the bounds of confidentiality), especially those whose judgment you trust (not including yes people who are likely to tell you what you want to hear). The perspective gained by this process will yield a working approximation of what a reasonable person in a like situation might view to be appropriate.

BUILD TRUST

You may have heard someone say, "You only have so many chips to play, so play them wisely." Nonsense. We do have to play our chips wisely, but we can gain new ones over time. Failure to do both is one reason (along with mobility, misfeasance, malfeasance, exhaustion, and burnout) why the tenure of administrators is short. The assessment, "He did a lot of good things, but he's burned all his chips," applies very well.

There are two basic ways to gain new chips: consistently passing the basic fairness test and treating people well. Different constituents will see basic fairness differently at any point in time. For example, if an appeal goes against the appellant, her supporters may view it as unfair while her department head thinks the decision was wisdom personified. In the short term, all must see it as neither arbitrary, nor capricious, nor discriminatory. In the long run, the collective reasonable person will view the facilitator, adjudicator, and mediator as basically fair.

It should not be necessary to remind people that they must treat others well, but it is. Some individuals can be interpersonal dolts even when they mean well, but they are rare. Sincerity generally comes through in the not-very-long-run. The most common problem here is egocentric arrogance. High-level administration can be an ego trip, more for some than others. Unfortunately, this can lead to situations where some people treat those above them with the utmost respect and those below them (in the institutional hierarchy) with little to none. The most important aspect of gaining new chips, in addition to basic fairness, is to treat everyone with sincere respect. This means everyone—the janitors, the president, board members, secretaries, all faculty (including those with whom you have a history of old disputes and disagreements).

DEVELOP INTERPERSONAL SKILLS AND COOLING-DOWN TECHNIQUES

Two emotions figure heavily into conflict: anger and fear. They commonly exist at the same time. Two or more people beset by anger and fear will fuel each other's fire, and the conflict will escalate. This can be a major problem face-to-face, but email or even the traditional memo is worse because it makes the conflict a matter of record. Thus, the first order of business is to cool down. This also will take the edge off the emotions of the other parties.

In conflict management and resolution, temper is a large liability. Some people have a hotter temper than others. Controlling one's temper is the first step toward dealing with this. Experts in the field prescribe a number of techniques, such as breathing and nonthreatening body language. These do work and are important. They also can lead to the next, most important step: Do not get angry in the first place.

The following example of the relationship between physiology and interpersonal communication is played out between a man and another species, but it portrays the idea in a very fundamental way. Behind the highly stylized horse whisperer in the movie by the same name (the book had it a little closer to reality), there are numerous examples of the real thing. One such person is Monty Roberts. The basic concept of Mr. Roberts' demonstrations is that he will take an unbroken two-year-old horse, a rider on his back, and put the horse through the basics without a big fuss in about 30 minutes. I have seen him do it, and it is amazing indeed. In one of Mr. Roberts' video demonstrations, he comes to a point where, for the first time, he is putting on the saddle and pulling up the girth under the chest of a two-year-old filly. This is the point where an explosion is most likely. Just then, Roberts emphasizes an idea that is critical to cooling-down techniques. He says that at this point in the process it is important for the trainer to keep his heart rate down.

This vividly illustrates two things. One is that an adrenalin rush in one being can precipitate or accentuate an adrenalin rush in another. The other is a representation of advancing from controlling the expression of an emotion, to not having that emotion in the first place. This is not to say that one can be effective as a completely dispassionate automaton. However, it does recognize the very important relationship between the emotions of one individual and the escalating emotional reaction of another.

If all else fails and emotions run away in a conflict situation, acknowledge that things have gotten out of hand and call time-out with a commitment to revisit the issue at a specific later time.

TIMING

There is much wisdom in the phrase "Timing is everything." While it applies well to politics, market dynamics, career opportunities, and just about everything else, it also has a great deal of importance in the prevention, resolution, and (rarely) management of conflict. Addressing disputes quickly and directly is usually successful and is almost always the best approach. Having said that, there are many times when a more measured strategy is best—even necessary. The two examples given below characterize such contrasting situations.

If a person has a burst of temper toward one or more individuals, or makes a rude or hurtful remark, albeit it intentional or unintentional, an apology (with or without an explanation) should be rendered as soon as possible, before the seed of discontent can germinate.

By contrast, if an individual comes forward with a story about some incident or collection of incidents that attributes inappropriate action to one or more individuals, it should be taken as important but not gospel. Never accept such stories as a complete set of facts. Fact-finding becomes the order of the day, even though it will take time. In such an instance, it is essential that the parties know immediately that the issue is being addressed. The right time to bring the matter to closure is as soon as practicable once the facts are known.

Another aspect of timing has to do with the order in which different individuals or groups need to be engaged or consulted. This is a critical issue in institution-wide dispute resolution or prevention. For example, if the provost is addressing institution-wide policy on guidelines for an upcoming distribution of new salary adjustment money, the sequence of events is critical. Assume she is working with the president and his staff, the deans, and the leadership of the faculty senate, with or without a bargaining unit. Allowing draft guidelines to appear in a faculty senate meeting before they have been discussed with the deans (who will have to oversee the actual distribution of funds in the colleges) will be highly problematic. Of course, it is essential that proper sequencing and fact-finding does not become a point of rationalization for procrastination.

Other examples of taking advantage of timing to minimize the likelihood of unproductive conflict are more nuanced. For example, a dean might be conducting a meeting in which a number of participants seated around a conference table are asked to give their assessment of an issue. Each person in turn gives an evenhanded, logical assessment until it is Joe's turn. Joe uses the occasion as an opportunity to make a caustic remark with reference to a related issue about which he has an axe to grind and about which he knows the dean holds a different view. The dean might jump in with a reflex rejoinder, precipitate a pointless argument, and come off looking like he took the bait. Or he might simply say that the last point tends to get off the subject and go on to the next person. Or if the remark requires a comment or a factual correction, she might decide to go on to two or three of the next participants, then return to Joe with something like "Joe, as I think about your remark on (such and such), a number of other key issues make your proposal unworkable for these reasons . . . ," and then proceed to the next participant. This makes it clear to everyone that the dean is not dodging the issue, that she thought about it rather than firing back an ill-considered retort, that Joe's remark is off the subject, and that the meeting is going ahead with the matter at hand.

Finally, it must be noted that some disputes cannot be resolved immediately. Some never can be resolved and fall into the management category. However, some of the most difficult conflicts that seem impossible to settle in anything like a routine manner can mature to the point that they can be solved at the last hour if those responsible for the effort stay in the game. This is a little like settling litigation on the courthouse steps. Most of these cases involve serious issues, like loss of livelihood or loss of reputation. When the parties have come close enough to the abyss to look into it and see how far they might fall, one or both is much more likely to signal a willingness to resolve the dispute. However, this moment can be seized only if the parties to the process still have their hands on the wheel and a relevant game plan in mind.

USE ALL APPROPRIATE RESOURCES

When individuals are given administrative responsibility, and with it the obligation to see that unavoidable problems are solved, sometimes they believe they have to do it all by themselves. One of the many values of a meaningful orientation and professional development program is to make clear that this is not the case. In fact, many resources are available at any institution of higher learning, and people with problem-solving responsibility must learn to use them effectively.

The admonition to seek help and ask for advice is not limited to institutional offices, such as the attorneys, ombudspersons, affirmation action, and so forth, but to individuals who have special experience, skills, and knowledge. These assets are particular to any given situation.

Other administrative officers or faculty colleagues are key sources of help. For example, if the provost is not sure he understands where the deans are coming from on a high-impact issue, he should ask them, collectively or individually, for their interpretation and advice (he should already have done so anyway). If the board or the president see the need to take a specific action that is likely to be controversial, the deans should be included in the discussion and their cooperation sought. The same is true for the faculty leadership. The president of the faculty senate should be, and usually is, very knowledgeable about how a given decision will impact the faculty or be seen by various factions. Care must be taken not to inadvertently put this individual in the position of seeming to be co-opted by the administration, but this can be acknowledged and a process established to eliminate it.

In institutions that have a bargaining unit, many of these issues are worked out between the administration or board and the unit, with greater or lesser involvement of the general faculty, for example through the faculty senate or its equivalent. At a superficial level, this can simplify the process. However, it also can render the faculty senate less effective and deprive the institution of the level of discourse and sometimes messy pushing, shoving, and arguing that is crucial to thoroughly considering a decision that will impact the future mission.

DO IT LIKE THEY DO BASKETBALL

Ten or fifteen years ago, I saw a video of a speech by Steve Jobs, chief executive officer of Apple Computer. One of the themes in Jobs' speech was on management by basketball. It has been valuable to me ever since, especially in recent years when applied to dispute resolution.

This idea resonates extremely well with the previous section on using all available resources. Put another way: Do not try to go it alone. Taken one step further, preventing, resolving, and managing conflict can be done far more effectively if a team approach can be used, rather than a simple referral system. Here is where Steve Jobs' idea comes in.

Like all team sports, basketball requires a mix of talent that can be rapidly adapted to changing situations. The team has to play a full-court game. They must play the whole game; they must get the ball to the player with the best chance to score in a given situation. Today, a team cannot be successful at a high level without at least eight players in the mix. Some have similar responsibilities, but they all have different specific strengths.

In dispute resolution, a given individual beset by all the stress and strain attached to serious conflict may signal a high level of confidence in one person who can become the key to getting things on track. Those responsible for the resolution process must be in a position to capitalize on this, so long as the person is constructive and discreet. Such an individual might be a regular member of an integrated dispute resolution group or someone entirely outside the established system. He might be a facilitator, a go-between, an advocate, or one who simply accompanies the disputant during key steps in the process of resolution. This individual can bring the ball down the court and pass it off to the individual(s) who is in a position to actually take the administrative steps necessary to reach resolution, but remain in the mix. If the issue can be kept in play until the right players get in the game, the dean and provost might be able to mount a fast break and get the issue resolved in a way that works for everyone.

Although it is true that increasing the number of people involved in solving a sensitive problem also increases the possibility of a breach of confidence, if the participants have been carefully selected in advance, the benefits far outweigh the risks.

Mentoring and Early Negative Tenure Decisions

On a person-by-person basis, many of the serious disputes occurring in colleges and universities have to do with young faculty and decisions about promotion and tenure. The really traumatic cases are usually those related to an up-or-out tenure decision. They should be rare, and there are two ways to make it so. One is through the development of and adherence to criteria, standards, and procedures for consideration for promotion and tenure. The other is through mentoring, including that which takes place in the annual evaluation and reappointment process.

If the criteria and standards are understood by all the parties and agreed upon procedures are followed, then it should be clear whether the probationer is making adequate progress. If not, she must receive clear and timely feedback as to how to improve. If improvement is not forthcoming in a timely way, she should be counseled out or not reappointed. An excellent way to ensure that this happens is to require an in-depth mid-probationary review in the third year of the probationary period. It is in no one's best interest to allow an assistant professor to proceed toward an up-or-out tenure and promotion decision if it is evident that he is not likely to be successful. If tenure is denied, valuable career development time is wasted, and the probationer's future options will be diminished significantly.

Sometimes, departmental faculty, department heads, deans, and chief academic officers try to get around the discomfort of not reappointing a tenure-track assistant professor by allowing tenure without promotion. In this author's view, this is an extremely bad practice. If criteria and standards are clear and agreed upon procedures are being followed, then the only reason tenure is likely to be denied is because the assistant professor either lacks the requisite talent or commitment or proves not to be a good match for the position. To tenure such an individual in the hope that he will improve to the point of someday becoming an associate professor is not fair to the candidate, and it definitely is not fair to the institution. In most, but admittedly not all, such instances, the newly tenured individual will consistently rank low in the annual evaluation process, resulting in minimal salary increases and continued disappointment. The resultant frustration will quickly lead to burnout and a chronic complainer is born. If the difficult decisions had been made early on, the individual might have found the right career match in another academic environment, the institution would have had the position filled with a much more productive faculty member, and an instance of chronic conflict would have been averted.

NEVER STOP IMPROVING THE EDUCATION AND INFORMATION PROGRAM

It is all too easy to make temporary progress, only to have it dissipate when other issues arise or when changes in leadership occur. Thus, a system and accompanying culture of dispute resolution must be established in a way that optimizes the chance of sustainability. The surest way to do this is to systematize administrator education and development, interaction among the dispute resolution group, and information access to faculty and staff. This need not cost a lot of money, but responsibility must be assigned for each of these areas, and the chief academic officer must take overall responsibility. Evaluation of administrators is an extremely important part of the education process. Candid self-assessment and feedback from supervisors, faculty, and staff is critical to improving skills in DPRM.

In most instances, the focal point of an ongoing training program should be department chairs and heads. It should be noted that if chairs cycle through their appointment on a three-year basis, especially in an election-based system, the likelihood of sustaining a critical mass of able individuals with experience in dispute resolution is diminished.

Appendix 1: The Evaluation

For the tenth time in the last week, Jeff Broderick picked up Tom Kramer's letter. He was so mad his hands were shaking. It was the so-called annual evaluation letter that would determine his salary adjustment for next year. In Jeff's mind, it also pronounced judgment on his professional worth, at least in the eyes of the new administration. At 59, he didn't seem to be worth much. Without reading the letter again, Jeff laid it on the growing pile of work yet to be completed, ranging from revision of a rejected manuscript on the Kiowa, Pueblo Indian controversy to partially graded final exams. He desperately wanted out of this job. He was almost old enough to retire, but the market had gone south and his account wouldn't support him now even if he was two or three years older. Add it all up and he was not just mad, he was scared. Suddenly, Broderick was aware that he had developed a nervous tic under his left eye.

He looked around his office. The floor-to-ceiling books on the east wall were a great collection. His old oak library desk was in front of a west window and, walking to it, he looked out over the campus. Broderick used to think there could be no better life than that of a tenured professor. He loved to watch the academic world go by, especially between classes when students were walking across the campus, backpacks flopping, butt packs bumping, chitchat flowing, more smoking now than 10 years ago. Now and again a bare bellybutton floated by on low-slung hip huggers. One bore a stainless steel ring. If Broderick lived to be a hundred, he never would decode the ring thing.

Movement on the second floor of Harold Hall caught his eye. Named for a long-deceased dean of the graduate school, Harold was an administrative annex, which included the affirmative action office. Marvin Fields, the director, had the windowsill up, filling a little terra cotta dish with dried corn for Fluffy, the red squirrel with whom he had a long-standing relationship. The glare on the glass obscured everything but the black hands with the tiny yellow nuggets streaming through the fingers, but in his mind's eye Broderick could see Fields' expressive face. Fields was the real McCoy; a guy you could ride the river with, as they say. Fluffy was at arm's length on the limb of a huge oak tree. His plumed tail twitched in anticipation. The system required that Fluffy jump from the limb to a large, dried up old vine that ran along Marvin's window, thence, with a skip and a hop to Marvin's windowsill and the corn dish. Broderick had been fascinated with the Fluffy/Marvin show for years. For all he knew, this was the tenth Fluffy. How long do squirrels live, anyway?

Broderick ran his hand over his face and realized he had forgotten to shave. His sparse gray hair was in disarray. The room was hot because the physical plant had not yet turned on the air conditioning for the summer, which was why he wore shorts to work. This particular pair had the added benefit of a deep crotch and high waistline that minimized his sagging belly. Suddenly, he made a decision. Grabbing the letter off his desk, he rushed out the door and headed for the department office.

Tom Kramer had been head of sociology and anthropology for a little under a year. The new dean of arts and sciences, Moira Barstow, had hired him from outside to get "some new blood in play" and strengthen the research and Ph.D. program without hurting the undergraduate programs, of course. Moira had been hired by the new provost, who had been hired by the (now almost) new president, so the whole chain of command was still getting its feet on the ground. Kramer had made his bones (he always thought the anthropologists would get a kick out of that, which they did not) as a sociologist by shedding new light on the impact of urbanization on the environment and local standard of living in the Midwest and Great Plains. He was a high-energy kind of guy with a quick mind and a lot of ideas, some of which were pretty good. It was clear to Kramer that a lot of grant money was out there to be pulled in. To do this, he needed to hire two or three key people and get a critical mass of the current faculty geared up and pushing a little harder, especially in grant writing and research. In turn, this had positive implications for taking the Ph.D. program up a level. The central administration and the dean had a lot of good things to say about these plans.

Kramer looked at his watch. Beads of sweat trickled from his salt and pepper sideburns. He was supposed to be at a department head meeting in 15 minutes. The dean was having all the heads (the ongoing debate about heads versus chairs notwithstanding) make presentations on the goals for their departments, along with a summation of fiscal and other implications. He was the first of four presenting today. A door slammed in the outer office. He heard voices, but couldn't catch the words. As he reached for his sport coat, Anna Coombs, the departmental secretary, appeared in the door. Kramer thanked God every day he had had the blind luck to inherit her when he began this job.

Anna was very perceptive, with a great sense of people. She had been courted, slighted, screamed at, praised and rewarded, in no particular order, through 15 years on the job. In her mind, the jury was still out on this Kramer fellow, but he had possibilities.

"I know you have a heads meeting in fifteen minutes," Anna said, "but Professor Broderick is out here and wants to see you."

She saw Kramer glance at his watch. "I told him you had a meeting, but he says it's important."

Kramer pulled on his jacket. "Let's try five minutes," he said. "If that doesn't do it, we can take it up later."

Broderick strode into the office, and Kramer could see he was upset. The red blotches on the man's neck were a dead giveaway, to say nothing of the nervous tic. He made a guess that this was about Broderick's evaluation and salary adjustment, or lack of one. Those shorts would appear better, Kramer thought to himself, if Broderick would leave the white socks at home. "What's up, Jeff?" he asked.

Broderick clutched the letter in his fist like a heavy weapon, jabbing it in Kramer's general direction. "We need to talk about this evaluation. I have been putting this off for weeks because I didn't want to cause trouble, but it just isn't right. If this is how we get treated for sticking it out in this place for a whole career, I guarantee you are going to spend the next three years tied up in one grievance after another—starting with me."

Kramer took a deep breath and counted to three. "Bad timing, Jeff," he replied. "That will take a lot longer than five minutes, and that's all I have right now."

"So when can we do it?"

"I'm going to be gone for a week, starting later today, to a conference in Arizona. Why don't you send me an email and sort of lay out the problem?"

"That," Broderick said, his face getting redder, "is nothing but a brush off. There's no reasonable way to deal with something like this in an email."

"Well," Kramer said, his voice rising with his temper, "it doesn't solve anything for you to come barging in here like a bull in a china closet expecting to get your problems solved on a moment's notice. You've had six weeks to bring this up." He paused and straightened his tie. "We'll deal with it when we both have time. Right now, I've got to get going."

With that, Kramer brushed past Broderick and left the man standing in his office. In his haste, he didn't see Anna Coombs roll her eyes and shake her head.

Kramer's presentation went well. In fact, several other heads said they might want to plagiarize a piece of it. The dean had a couple of minor suggestions and asked for a little more detail in the faculty qualification and financial components. The meeting ran long, though, and he very nearly missed his flight to Phoenix. Looking back on it, hunkered down in seat 12A flying into an artificially extended sunset, Kramer felt good about the dean's meeting and bad about his encounter with Broderick who could be very engaging one minute and aggravating the next. He was not without depth, having won a couple of college-level teaching awards, but he never brought in a dime and hadn't published a paper in five years. For all Kramer knew, Broderick had never written a grant proposal in his life. He could not see how the man was going to be any kind of force in taking the department up a level. Something kept nagging at him, though, that he couldn't quite put his finger on. A flight attendant came by and he ordered a glass of dry red wine, which turned out to be a screw top split of cabernet, complete with a plastic glass.

As Kramer sipped his wine, the elderly man in the middle seat paged through *Newsweek*. Reading over the man's shoulder, so to speak, Kramer thought to himself that every headline in the whole issue had to do with terrorism, airline security, the declining stock market, or a combination thereof. He thought for a moment that his own retirement account had declined about a third, then decided that with 25 years to go before he hung it up, he wouldn't worry about it, at least not now.

Kramer dozed off; his wine perched precariously on the fold-down table. A spate of choppy air jarred him awake. As he saved his wine from splashing onto his shirtfront, the pilot was announcing that Albuquerque could be seen from the left-hand side of the plane. Sure enough, there it was, like a handful of diamonds thrown across the black expanse of desert. Broderick was on his mind again. He remembered that when he called the office on his way to the airport, Anna had said, in a kind of off-hand way, that he really was a pretty good sort. She also allowed as how the students just loved the guy. Kramer had begun to think that people like Broderick, who seemed disconnected from where the university was headed, might be scared out of their wits. They couldn't adapt and they couldn't retire, at least not now. Well, that wasn't his problem. He looked out again into the night and watched Albuquerque slide under the plane's left wing. On the other hand, maybe it was very much his problem.

The next morning at 9:30, Jeff Broderick was at his desk plowing through final exams. He felt better but didn't know why. A row with your boss is supposed to be a bummer, but it seemed like a big weight had been lifted off his solar plexus. When he left Kramer's office, he had been furious. Anna, who he regarded as a pretty cagey lady, had told him to go home and cool off. On the way out, she also reminded him he had to get his final grades in this afternoon. This morning, he had shaved and put on a crisp, starched shirt. His wife had told him he looked like a doofus with his white athletic socks and shorts, and "for God's sake, just leave the socks in the drawer." As usual, she was right. Somehow or other, he felt a little more together. In a small way, he seemed more in control.

The phone rang. To Broderick's surprise, it was Kramer. "Jeff, this is Tom Kramer."

There was a moment of silence, then "Oh, hi. This is a surprise, I thought you were in Arizona."

"I am. Look, let's call time out from yesterday and start over. I apologize for rushing off. I had my mind on a presentation I had to make in 10 minutes and just didn't stop and think. Let's set a specific time to get together when I get back and take however long we need to really get this sorted out."

"I'm up for that," Broderick replied, "but what about my salary? The budget is pretty well a done deal, I would think." What's going on here, he thought to himself. Is this guy schizophrenic or what?

"If changes are made, and I am not saying they will be, we can handle that retroactively, one way or another. Look, I'm not promising anything, but I do want to commit to being sure we really give your concerns the attention they deserve."

Well, I'll be damned, Broderick thought to himself. "That works for me," he said.

Broderick hung up and leaned back in his chair. Then he got up and checked Marvin Field's window. No Fluffy and no Marvin. He sat back down and attacked the exam grading again. In a few minutes, he was so absorbed that he failed to notice Adelle Sweet standing in the door of his office. In fact, she knocked twice to get his attention.

"Oh, hello, Dr. Sweet," Broderick said, bouncing off his rickety swivel chair. He offloaded a pile of paper from the one other seat in his office. "Have a chair."

Adelle was a star. She had been hired as a tenure-track associate professor three years ago, been tenured after two years, and likely would be a full professor in a couple more. Broderick had a suspicion that the only way the university had been able to get her was that her mother was not well and lived 60 miles away. She was an archeologist on her way up. Adelle had just received notice that she had a three-year grant for $276,000 to survey a possible pre-Clovis site in southern California. For whatever the reason, Broderick and Sweet kind of hit it off, having similar interests on a number of fronts. More to the point, they were two of only five people in the anthropology section, one of whom was primarily occupied with forensic work. She could be pretty perceptive and was always straightforward. Broderick had noticed that she talked to Anna Coombs quite a bit. After all, there were no other women in the department.

"Sometimes," Adelle said, "I get the impression you're pretty frustrated with research. Tell me if I'm being too nosey."

Broderick did a quick assessment. If he could dust this for prints, he suspected he would find Anna Coombs's somewhere along the edges. He leaned back in his chair and looked at the ceiling. Then he looked at the floor. Then he looked at Adelle. "I really believe I am a solid scholar in my field. I have done some pretty respectable work on the economy and demographics of 18th and 19th century high plains Indians. I bet I know more about that subject than all but four or five other people in the country."

"I'll vouch for that. I know enough historic Indian stuff to make some judgment about it. Why don't you write more? You have, what, five or six papers? Have you ever had a grant?"

Broderick folded his arms across his chest and slid a few inches down in his chair. He wanted to say that in the first years of his career here, grants didn't matter. He would like to have described the long hours he had spent wrestling with proposals, some of which were mailed, none of which were funded. Most of all, he was itching to tell her about the passion he had developed for teaching as he grew older and to remind her of his teaching awards. But, he figured, she would just point out how teaching was a refuge for people that couldn't get the grants or publications. Finally, he just said "Nope."

Adelle clicked her nails on the arm of her chair. She knew full well Broderick was a true scholar in his specialty. She also knew he was truly a good, even outstanding, teacher, at least when he wasn't in a funk. She'd heard he drank too much beer, but hadn't seen it firsthand. And of most immediate relevance, she knew she had a time problem with meeting her commitments to the grant.

"You know," she said, "I have this grant starting in July. It's going to have me out of town some, especially next spring, getting organized for the on-site work next summer. That's going to have me in a bind with teaching Intro to Archeology in the spring semester. This is bound to get worse in years two and three. I'm going to have a lot of samples and data to deal with. To really make it go, we need graduate students. The anthropology Ph.D. has slid into near oblivion. Without resuscitation and better definition as an interdisciplinary program, it's going to be eliminated. To build it back to respectability, one of the things we need is a graduate seminar in the broad outlines of early Americans spanning from Clovis man to European contact. We also need more faculty with Ph.D.s. We can get collaborators from geology. I have some feelers out there. Al French wants to work with us in dating and strata. So, the bottom line is, I need a collaborator who is a strong teacher. I thought you might be interested."

Angels were singing, or at least one angel. Broderick thought for a moment that he had glimpsed the threshold of heaven. How could this be possible? Then he had a glimpse of reality as well. "Look," he said, "this is really great stuff. I appreciate it, and I can see the logic. But how can this work for me? You cannot imagine how much I would love an arrangement like you just described. And I guarantee I can deliver, both in the undergrad course and in the graduate seminar. But I won't be doing research or publishing, and that is going to get me low evaluations and no raises."

Adelle had expected this and knew it to be true. "Maybe we can convince Kramer and the dean to buy it. You truly are an outstanding teacher. I know that. And you really know your stuff, whether you write about it or not. Look, I can't build on this grant by myself. To create a bigger, better graduate program around grants and research I need more time. I don't see the department hiring another anthropologist. But if you take on some of my teaching and we do a first-class graduate seminar together, I can get several doctoral students involved in my survey and we're on our way."

Broderick thought about it for a moment, but no longer. "I'm in," he said. "I am supposed to have a meeting with Kramer when he gets back. Let me get him thinking about it. If there is any sign of support, we can follow up with a two on one. We'll outnumber him."

Adelle Sweet smiled. "I think the support will come," she said, "but if not, we won't stop there."

And so it came to pass that Tom Kramer, Adelle Sweet, and Jeff Broderick met with Dean Barstow three weeks later. They had a proposal for building the research base and graduate program in anthropology, and they were enthusiastic about it, even though it still was pretty sketchy.

Broderick himself, thinking back on the meeting with the dean, had to be impressed. Moira Barstow had been in the job for just over a year, but she came to it with a lot of experience and a real feel for solving people problems. He had met her only in passing before the meeting. He recalled that as he and Tom Kramer and Adelle Sweet sat down with her in her office, he had misgivings. They had the framework for a solution, but it was not firm and she had to buy into it—literally.

Dressed in a power suit complete with a scarf folded under her jacket, she reminded Jeff of the IBM yellow pokadot tie and gray flannel suit stereotype of days gone by. But she came across as feminine, approachable, and professional, all at the same time. She arranged them around a table in the corner of her office, by the window. The view of the campus was a classic. Students streamed by between classes, which reminded them of why they were all there in the first place. She had flowers in the center of the table, but they were short enough to see over. Once they got through a little lets-get-reacquainted chitchat, she framed the question that guided the meeting: "Well, folks, what do we each want to get out of this?"

The conversation immediately began to ramble with problems and partial solutions getting jumbled together. After a few minutes of this, she called time out and asked everyone to answer the question individually, starting with Kramer. He allowed that he was hired to build the research base of the department and its graduate programs without letting the undergraduate program slide. To do that he needed new resources, but he also needed the existing faculty to take it up a notch. He thought the three of them had some ideas that could help make that happen. He also said that although he needed additional faculty positions, he didn't see them being in anthropology. The dean said they would get back to solutions in a few minutes. Adelle Sweet said she could bring in grants, do good research, and publish. She already had proven that. She also could recruit and train more and better Ph.D. candidates. But she couldn't do it alone. The demands were too great for her to keep her undergraduate teaching assignment on track. She had to have help. Broderick said that for starters, he wanted respect. He expected to earn it, but he wanted a clear shot at being a contributor and being rewarded if he succeeded. He also wanted to take a stronger role in teaching. He loved it, was good at it, and, to be candid, was not all that enthused about research, partly because he had not proved to be very successful at it. Dean Barstow said she had very limited resources with which to meet very high expectations and had to leverage her money and get results. Anthropology might not be a top priority, but it was not at the bottom either.

"All right," the dean said. "Now let's talk about some options. I think you have some ideas, and I have a few of my own. We need to see how some of these match up with our interests. Tom, start us off."

At the end of another hour, an agreement was struck in principle. The deal was that the dean would find the money for a graduate research assistant for Dr. Sweet and support it for three years, by which time Dr. Sweet was to have grant funding to carry it. There also had to be at least four doctoral candidates working with her and Jeff Broderick by then. These were to be funded by grants or indirect cost recovery. She would work with Kramer, Sweet, and the head of the geology department to designate more officially Al French's role in the anthropology Ph.D. Dr. Broderick was to take on an additional undergraduate course, specifically Dr. Sweet's Introduction to Archeology, and take the lead in the graduate seminar on Clovis to contact. That meant three undergraduate courses each semester plus the graduate seminar. An additional 800-level course would have to be developed, and they would work on this together with a one-year deadline. In addition to the research assistant for Dr. Sweet, Dr. Broderick would have a graduate teaching assistant. In this arrangement, he would be evaluated according to criteria and standards based on the work he was doing. He and Tom Kramer were to develop these and bring them to the dean for approval. These included the necessity for him to contribute to the body of knowledge about anthropology, but this could be in the form of refereed papers in his field of interest or in teaching anthropology, or both. A minimum of five publications by the end of three years was established as an expectation. The entire program would be evaluated at the end of four years and that process would include bringing in an outside consultant as an evaluator.

DISCUSSION

This fictionalized scenario is a somewhat idealized composite of many real cases. Most readers will immediately recognize this story in its many forms. It is a very common situation, recreated here to show what well-intended people can do to bring about constructive resolution of a divisive and destructive situation.

In this instance, a little coaching and counseling converged with interest-based negotiation to bring about a positive effect, idealized though it may be. Importantly, no one announced himself to be a counselor or a facilitator or an interest-based negotiator. People who really wanted to solve a problem and get ahead simply brought those principles into play. With the exception of the dean, no one at the meeting had even read about them.

One of the key elements is that at least two people saw the need to bring water to a fire rather than gasoline. If Anna Coombs had started a hallway gossip campaign about the new department head's blowup with Jeff Broderick instead of keeping it in confidence, much damage would have been done. She planted a hardy seed in Adelle Sweet's fertile mind by mentioning that Broderick might make a good collaborator for a strong researcher. And it didn't hurt anything that she mentioned in passing to Tom Kramer that Broderick really was a nice person at heart and that the students loved him.

Tom Kramer, even though he had a pretty short fuse and large ego, had the depth of character to take the initiative and call Broderick about starting over. He was willing to apologize about the first encounter in the interest of getting things back on track. Whether he did these things out of altruism or because he realized it was in his own enlightened self-interest matters not. He also demonstrated the ability to think out of the box, or at least to consider a new idea.

Adelle Sweet showed real ability to innovate and see how the parts of a bigger picture might fit together. She had the confidence to take the initiative and visit Broderick with an idea. She treated him with respect, the one thing for which he hungered most. She saw that by solving this problem, she was also furthering her own interests. She has the makings of a very good dean some day, once she gets her full professorship.

Jeff Broderick was willing to recognize that he wasn't meeting the kind of expectations consistent with the effort to take the level of anthropology up a notch. While he might not have agreed with the new priorities, he recognized their reality. Instead of going into a permanent bunker mentality, he demonstrated receptivity to carrying his end of a new approach. This was a serious emotional ride for Broderick. Without some support on the home front and several fair-minded colleagues, he might well have been forced into a poverty-ridden early retirement, ill health, or both. Of course, if he doesn't perform on his end of the agreement, that could happen anyway. But I have confidence in him.

The whole process might have been handled more easily, or even been prevented, if the department had a set of procedures, criteria, and standards outlining how people could contribute to the mission according to their strengths. Criteria and standards for Dr. Broderick's individual performance expectations had to be created ad hoc. For this to work for more people in the long term, the university would have to develop overarching policy encouraging and supporting it. In this instance, Dr. Broderick was already a full professor based on standards that had prevailed long ago but were no longer relevant to the new circumstances. If he had been an associate professor, the criteria and standards that were created would have had to have been related to the possibility, or lack, of eventual promotion to full professor.

In a perfect world, Dr. Broderick might have become a mirror image (professionally speaking) of Dr. Sweet, but that is not how the world works. But the total productivity resulting from this arrangement, assuming it is faithfully implemented, will be far greater than if Broderick spent his last working years in a perpetual funk and Adelle Sweet struggled to do a marginal job of meeting the obligations on her grant.

Appendix 2: A Matter of Intractable Conflict

Janice Fillmore was a very happy woman. She was about to leave North Valley University to become dean of arts and sciences at another institution. She had loved her time at North Valley, in part because she learned so much. Her time as head of a large department had been very fulfilling. She knew she would call on every one of her experiences in the new job. Certain basic themes stood out in her reflections. These were to help everyone grow and empower people according to their strengths; to communicate as clearly and as often as humanly possible; to have a strategy and stay ahead of the curve. She had also learned that sometimes, albeit rarely, some faculty might want to create problems instead of solve them, and it was essential to neutralize those situations as quickly and constructively as possible.

Eight Years Earlier

Fred Wallace was new to the job. Serving as head of the Department of English in the arts college at North Valley University for five months had changed his life—mostly for the worse. He had the headaches and high blood pressure to prove it. A nationally recognized scholar in 17th century English literature, Fred had arrived in mid-August as the new head of a department with 21 faculty members and about 40 teaching assistants (TAs). Many of these individuals were working on a master's of arts degree in his department. There were a few doctoral candidates too, but enrollment in the Ph.D. program had dropped in recent years.

Fred brought a big dose of scholastic firepower to the program. That was the main reason he was hired. He had precious little experience in administration—none, in fact. He was being baptized by fire, through immersion in a budget reduction that had not been mentioned in his interview and an enrollment surge that outstripped faculty and TA numbers. At least this was so under the historical definition of teaching load at North Valley.

Wallace was learning about his faculty. Upon his arrival, he had initiated a series of one-on-one meetings, starting with the professorial ranks. He recognized the need to get acquainted and identify the department's strengths and weaknesses as soon as possible. It was clear there were more strengths than weaknesses, but individual specialties were all over the map. There was no real critical mass in any specific area. Fred had begun to suspect that was the real reason the doctoral program was crashing. He encountered special opportunities to learn about two faculty members in particular: Marcus Jones and Delbert Baronne, both full professors. So far, one thing was clear—they hated each other. Wallace had never before encountered two people with such a diabolical combination of personalities.

The trouble with Baronne was that he was a conniving, self-serving snake, bent on taking credit for everything good that happened and undermining Jones whenever the opportunity presented itself—according to Jones.

The problem with Jones, or at least the biggest problem, was his temper. Well, his temper and his tendency to lie about everything connected with Baronne—according to Baronne.

It was now mid-December. Christmas was looming. Parties were cropping up. The rumor mill was grinding at a furious pace. Nerves were frayed. It had taken Wallace a month or so to realize the intensity of the Baronne and Jones dynamic. Every time he peeled back one layer, another spiny, prickly encrustation emerged.

This was due in part to the striking difference in the way the two men operated, not to mention their personalities. His first encounter, albeit indirect, had been with Marcus Jones. The man had barged into the department office on Wallace's second day in the job, insisting to see him—then! Wallace had been out, supervising the unloading of the moving van. More specifically, he and his wife were trying to decide what to do with all the "stuff" they could not find room for and wished they had left in Massachusetts.

When Audrey Peterson, the departmental secretary, could not give him a specific time to come back, Jones had jumped down her throat. Leaning over her desk, close enough that a drop of spittle landed on the crystal of Audrey's watch, Jones had stated in bitter, biting tones, "Well, are we going to have to put up yet again with an inaccessible chair? This department is coming unraveled before our very eyes. Do we have no one taking charge?"

Audrey had wiped her watch with a Kleenex, looking Jones in the eye. In a level voice, she told him to go scream at someone else. She had had her quota for the day. Something about the smoky intensity in her gray eyes shut him up and he left, slamming the door.

Skinny fit Jones better than trim. There was a hawk-like (detractors used a ferret metaphor) characteristic about him. He capitalized on this at times, to intimidate lesser folk. This was reinforced when needed by a very volatile temper, which had ceased to have much effect on the unflappable Audrey.

The reason Jones was in such a snit, Audrey opined to Wallace the next day, was something Professor Baronne reportedly had said about him in an email to a graduate student. How she knew this was a mystery. Fred would come to learn that Audrey had a phenomenal intelligence network that yielded mostly accurate information. At all events, Wallace made one of his first mistakes. He let the incident go. Fred was anxious to get off to a good start with his faculty. The slate was clean. He was looking forward to the job. He did not want to start off with a dispute. Wallace also would come to learn that Audrey Peterson, good soul that she was, could be the grand mistress of understatement. "They don't get on well," she had said.

Fred Wallace was an easygoing fellow with a laid-back style. He favored contact lenses for distance, complemented by reading glasses for close work. This enabled him to look outdoorsy in the lodge at Copper Mountain, but bookish (he preferred scholarly) in academic company. Sometimes he wore a beard and sometimes not. His wife had suggested to him more than once that the beard surfaced when he felt strung out and was shaved away when he was on a roll.

His introduction to Delbert Baronne came the next day. Baronne had an appointment for one of the get-acquainted sessions. They met in Wallace's office. Baronne was friendly, bordering on ingratiating. His sandy hair and freckles went with his stout form to create an impression of understated sincerity. The professor spoke at length about his research, a teaching award he had won the previous year, and a paper he would be presenting later in the fall. He gave his own version of where the department was strong and where it needed improvement. Baronne had a knack for compelling logic. He offered to provide any help he could. About the time Fred pulled in his driveway that night, he realized that Baronne had controlled the entire conversation.

On his way out, Professor Baronne said, in a confiding manner, "I probably ought to let you get your bags in the attic before bringing this up, but then I don't want you to get blindsided either." He paused to rub the edge of Wallace's desk with the ball of his thumb. "You need to keep your ear to the ground with the graduate students. There is some unrest, I would say, with the TAs. Quite a lot, I'm afraid. One of the graduate students told me a couple of days ago that some of the most influential among them are being encouraged to unionize."

That was new information. "By whom?" Wallace wanted to know.

"He didn't say. It just seemed like one more little spark out there. We certainly do not need the graduate students on the warpath, being understaffed the way we are."

Baronne again headed for the door, as if to really leave this time, but stopped with his hand on the doorknob. "Just a personal impression," he said to Wallace's computer screen, "but I think some of that is fueled by the enrollment slide in the Ph.D. program. There is some talk, you know, by the board, of eliminating underenrolled graduate programs. Or at least people say there is."

Baronne had departed, leaving in his wake a gracious word to Audrey, which she ignored, and Wallace had gone on with his day. Forty-eight hours later, three graduate students appeared. Their mission was of two parts. First, they were representing all the TAs in protesting the class size being imposed in Expository Writing I and II. They knew this was the result of budget cuts and enrollment increases, and they might have let it go, except that they were getting no salary increase and their pay was already obscenely low.

Wallace knew all this. It had been the same at his previous institution and was commonplace in universities; a problem made ever worse by the nonstop tightening of budgets. He did not have ready answers, at least not ones that these students wanted to hear. Another underlying cause, long since built into the financial structure of the institution, was that revenue from low-cost, lower-division courses, taught with low-cost labor in the form of graduate teaching assistants, made high-cost, upper-division courses, taught by real faculty, possible. Beyond raw economics, the rationale was that the TAs, when properly trained and supervised, gained teaching experience that was essential to their future aspirations.

Chip Masterson, a Ph.D. candidate, led off. Masterson was a tall kid with longish hair and a weedy looking moustache. He wore khaki shorts and a Grateful Dead T-shirt. His deeply imprinted Birkenstocks integrated his outfit with the culture.

"We know you are brand new," he started off, "but we wanted to get to you before you had been subjected to too much propaganda."

Masterson paused, either for effect, or because he was more nervous than he let on. "We've had it up to here," he continued, indicating the bottom of his chin. He looked at the two other students for confirmation. "Not only are we working harder, without competitive salaries and no raises, we don't have access to affordable health insurance. Worse yet, we don't even get a tuition break. We can't tell if we are students, employees, or serfs."

Masterson paused and leaned back in his chair, tugging at his mustache. With a glance, he tagged one of his team members, a female colleague whose name was Amy West. Amy was bright and pretty, with a chatty, engaging manner. Perky came to mind.

"We feel like serfs," she said. "We work our backsides off. Some of us have problems finding a major professor or even getting a graduate committee together. Quite a few are getting shortchanged as students. And you had just as well know that the general view is that this is all antecedent to ditching the Ph.D. program."

"Some of us were talking to Dr. Baronne a few days ago," Masterson continued. "He says quite a few of the faculty think we should unionize. That might help us help you put more pressure on the dean and the university to get more resources in the English department. It seems to us like that would be good for everyone, including the faculty."

Baronne, Wallace recalled, had made no reference at all to talking to the graduate students about a union himself. "Look," he replied, "I have a meeting coming up with the dean in a few days. I will bring all this to his attention and see what the possibilities are. Let me have that conversation and get back to you. While I am at it, I will try to find out more specifics about the real situation with the doctoral program."

"I might add," he continued, "that you generally get better results stating your case and working with people than fighting with them. I appreciate the opportunity to discuss this."

Wallace prearranged another meeting with the students for the day after his upcoming session with Dean Adams. He wasn't sure where this was headed, but it did not feel good. He also remembered his earlier conversation with Audrey Peterson about her encounter with Marcus Jones and his ire about an email Baronne had allegedly sent to "some graduate students."

"By the way," Wallace said, as the students were leaving, "have you discussed this with other faculty? Dr. Jones, maybe, or anyone else?"

"Thanks for bringing that up," Amy West answered. "That's a very sore point. Apparently Dr. Jones is not going to teach his 800 level course this fall—at the very last minute—and that is putting several students in a significant bind."

Since when, Wallace thought, did the faculty unilaterally decide when they were not going to teach a course? According to the course schedule, Jones was committed to teach it. "What do you base that on?" he asked.

Sue Morton, to this point the silent member of the delegation, spoke up. Sue was tall, even rangy. She looked hard as nails, but striking. He would later learn that she was a part-time coach of the women's crew team. She was about to finish her Ph.D. after nine years of slogging away at it. "I am really affected by this," she said, "so I looked into it. My major professor, Dr. Fillmore, said she had heard Jones was not teaching his graduate course this fall. Amy and I saw Dr. Baronne in the hall and asked him if he knew anything about it. He emailed us a couple of hours later and said he had heard Dr. Jones might even stop teaching it altogether."

Wallace asked the obvious question. "Have any of you actually talked to Dr. Jones about this?"

Masterson answered for all of them. "Not likely," he said. "He's jumped down our throats so many times about so many different things that we avoid him like the plague. Life is too short to absorb any more of his punishment than we have to." He paused, as if considering how far to go with this. "Sorry to tell you that," he added. "But that's just the way it is."

With that, the students left. Fred decided that, overall, he had had a lousy day so far. It was about to get worse.

As Wallace followed the students out of his office, who should be seated by Audrey's desk waiting to strike, but Marcus Jones. Smelling trouble, and guessing that Jones had overhead Masterson's scathing indictment, the students beat it for the door. Audrey peered up at Wallace, her brown eyes pleading innocence. "Dr. Jones would like to have a word with you, Dr. Wallace," she said. And so, instead of having an hour to run his email and wade into the pile of accrued paperwork on the corner of his desk, Wallace led Jones into his office and, somewhat apprehensively, invited him to have a seat.

Wallace's guest perched on the edge of his chair, hands clenched on his knees. His face was white, except for a red spot on each cheek and a blotch on the left side of his neck. Wallace could see the man's jaw muscles clenching beneath his sallow skin. He noticed that Jones was nearing baldness but had several strands of long black hair wound around his narrow peak. At a glance, the bare skin hardly showed.

"What you just heard from those students," Jones began in a thin, reedy voice, seething with tension, "is a direct reflection of the many problems that plague this department. We have too little money, too few faculty, too few graduate assistants, too many undergraduate students, and too many people bent on their own personal agenda. We are going to lose the Ph.D., which may be a blessing, because we no longer can afford to staff it."

Jones paused for breath and scooted back in his chair. His first blast delivered, he leaned back and closed his eyes. He tilted his head to the ceiling, then to the floor, rubbing his temples. "That student was right," he went on. "I heard the whole thing, of course. I have jumped several TAs, sometimes pretty hard. In fact, I really crawled all over a couple of them during summer school. What you haven't heard is why."

There was a long pause. "OK," Wallace said. "Why?"

Jones looked at Wallace—but not quite. He peered in his general direction, but more over his right shoulder. "No one is really working with our graduate students," he went on. "They get no training, no mentoring; they are stretched too far. As a consequence, a few of them are doing a lousy job with the undergrads, especially in Expository I. Faculty in other writing-intensive majors are starting to complain that the students they get from us can't write a simple sentence. When I find TAs slacking off, I jump their case. They don't like it."

He took another breather. "We also have a few faculty," he went on, "one in particular, who doesn't like me, and tries to use the students' discontent to get at me. In fact, he was in your office a couple of days ago, spreading venom about me, I have no doubt."

"If you mean Professor Baronne," Wallace responded, "he never mentioned your name."

"Be that as it may, his fingerprints are all over this. The man is evil, we had just as well be clear about that. It would be just like Baronne to stir up trouble with the graduate students, create a crisis, then come to see you and offer to help solve it. In doing so, he will use the opportunity to stab his many adversaries in the back," Jones seethed. "Me in particular."

Thus went Fred Wallace's introduction to the Baronne and Jones phenomenon. Seldom had he witnessed such intense dislike and venomous outpouring as Jones displayed. On the other hand, there was something about Baronne's glib manner that left him even more off center.

Throughout the fall, one issue followed another with increasing intensity. The two men dominated and disrupted one faculty meeting after another. On more than one occasion, Jones blew a gasket and stormed out, leaving Wallace feeling as if he was losing control of the situation, which he was. Baronne, in a subtle way, built factions among the graduate students and TAs, using issues such as teaching loads, class size, and compensation. Wallace's thoughts were in disarray. So many issues and bits of information and disinformation were flying about that in the discordant atmosphere that prevailed, he could not seem to get all the disparate parts connected.

The faculty split further, based on speculation and very few facts, over what to do about the Ph.D. The board had discussed it, but deferred further consideration of degree discontinuance until the next fall. Baronne represented himself as the standard bearer of the graduate students generally and the TAs in particular. He championed the Ph.D., which Jones asserted with fiery rhetoric that the department could not afford to maintain. He and Jones clashed frequently and severely on the subject of instructional quality, TA loads, faculty loads, the value of research, and the loss of research time in exchange for heavier teaching commitments. When the question of whether the department should launch a campaign to keep the Ph.D. came up, these issues were all rolled into that one dispute, and it became a straw man for their respective positions on other matters.

Most worrisome of all was one very serious, new development. The two key combatants held opposite views on whether a young Hispanic man should receive tenure and promotion. This was leveraging the fault line that already split the faculty. Hector Rodriguez, the individual on the bubble, was all too aware of the growing situation. He had been to see Wallace twice and had made an exploratory visit to the Office of Affirmative Action. He felt he had become a symbol of the animosity between Baronne and Jones.

Baronne believed (or said he believed) that Rodriguez had shown no evidence of developing a body of work in his area of specialty, contemporary Mexican-American literature, and that he had too many problems in the classroom. Jones asserted that Rodriguez had made huge improvements in his teaching, as evidenced by student ratings and his own observations from sitting in on his classes. He also argued that in addition to work from his dissertation, Rodriguez had published four papers in respected journals and was starting to receive invitations to speak at conferences.

"It must be kept in mind," he would assert, "that Hector's area of interest is an emerging field. It is much more difficult for him to become established in a traditional department."

"Even if one grants that possibility," Baronne had responded in a recent meeting, "one still has to ask if his area of study is all that relevant, at least to this department. We are already spread too thin across too many isolated areas in which we are one deep. This is always a danger with affirmative action hires."

Janice Fillmore, who generally did not say much, plunged into the fray, even before Jones could get started. "That is just appalling," she snapped. "We all knew what Hector's specialty was when he was hired. We didn't object then. It is outrageous and indefensible to criticize it now. In addition, many of us have complimented him at one time or another about his work with the Hispanic Student Alliance. We have several Hispanic English majors now, where we never did before. That takes time out of every day. We can't turn around now and penalize him for being short on publications."

Fillmore paused, realizing she was burning a lot of powder. "And another thing," she went on. "To refer to Hector Rodriguez as an 'affirmative action hire' is unacceptable. It is offensive, hurtful, and mean spirited. It also is false. We examined Hector's credentials very critically. He was in the top half dozen of the people we looked at."

Baronne looked around the table. His sandy hair slightly ruffled, his earnest expression matched by his sincerity of tone, he looked like God's own servant. "Granted that those are issues. It still is the case that with budget cuts continuing, the doctoral program at risk, and with undergraduate enrollments going up, we have to make every position count. We cannot afford to have someone doing half a job and sweep it under the rug in the name of diversity. Forgive me if I seem insensitive, but I'm just trying to be practical."

In the last 30 minutes, no one had spoken except Jones, Baronne, and Fillmore. The other tenured faculty members sat around the table. Some were listening, others were doodling; all were visibly frustrated.

Wallace saw Marcus Jones's neck turn red and his upper lip quiver. That always preceded an eruption. This had gone on long enough. He would like to have known more about how the other senior faculty members were reacting. From one-on-one discussions, he knew that most were capable, solid thinkers. But they seemed to be in the habit of letting Baronne and Jones take the role of discussants. In any event, it was almost five o'clock. Fred Wallace liked to let people have their say, but this was going nowhere.

"Let's leave it at that for now," he said. "I think everyone has a feel for what the issues are. This will be coming to a vote soon—within two weeks. Thank you all for your comments. Have a good weekend."

Wallace now had the vote of the tenured faculty on Hector Rodriguez's tenure and promotion in hand. They were split, as he had assumed, with nine voting no and six voting yes. The reasons given on the ballots reflected all the foregoing discussions and arguments. The views and votes split along lines generally framed by Baronne and Jones. With large misgivings, he had supported the majority of the faculty. Presently, the case was in the dean's hands, with his recommendation to go to the provost in a few days. He was aware that the dean had been over the case with his advisory council, and (courtesy of Audrey) that they also were split.

So now, in mid-December, Wallace stood looking out of his office window, unconsciously stroking his beard. An occasional student walked by in ankle deep snow, headed for one of the few remaining final exams. Fred had hit a new low. Earlier in the afternoon, the dean had come by with a copy of an anonymous computer fax. Someone had mastered the art of blitzing large listservs with anonymous email that was difficult, if not impossible, to trace. The missile had been sent to the president of the faculty senate, with shown copies to the president of North Valley University, each member of the board of regents, and the provost. The anonymous mailer had thrown in a copy to the governor for good measure, along with God knew who else. The governor had sent her copy to the board office and the board's executive director had sent it to the North Valley president with a request for information, even though the letter was unsigned. Wallace was disgusted that any attention at all was being paid to an anonymous letter.

However, the dean, being a pragmatist, noted, "Whoever did this could barrage the governor, legislature, board, donors, newspaper editors, and the general public with this sort of thing for months. And, believe me, eventually that can do a lot of damage, signed or not."

The upshot of the discussion was that they were getting together later this afternoon to hash it over. For about the tenth time, Wallace reread the offending epistle.

Dr. Miles Crumm
President, Faculty Senate
1214 Chamberlain Hall
Campus

Dear President Crumm:

We write to express alarm about events in the English department. Unfortunately, we will not be signing this letter because of the retribution we are certain to experience were we to do so.

Circumstances in the English department reflect the lack of vision and complete absence of communication that characterize the entire administration at this university. However, it has reached epic proportions in English. The damage is severe and growing. Factions have become armed camps. People are being hurt. The career of at least one tenure candidate is being destroyed. His candidacy has become a battleground of personal agendas. The students, especially graduate students, are being used as pawns. At least one faculty member is using them as foils, and the candidate's tenure decision as a stalking horse, to wage a battle over personal issues.

The department head is an inept coward. He has lost control of the situation and has no clue how to regain it, or even where to start.

The dean is an authoritarian hack of the president and provost. He has made things far worse by arbitrarily and capriciously withholding funds from the English department, which is critical to the university's ability to properly serve the ever-increasing number of new undergraduate students.

Students are the big losers. They cannot get into classes they need because sections are being cut. The undergrads feel disenfranchised and the graduate students are on the warpath. The teaching assistants are trying to create a union.

Something has to be done and soon. Your urgent attention to this matter will be appreciated by a large number of concerned faculty members.

Concerned Citizens of the University

Wallace liked to think he was not a coward. However, the anonymous author(s) had one thing right: He did not know where to start to get the situation back in hand. Still stamping snow off his feet, he stepped into Dean Frank Adams' office.

Adams had been dean for 15 years. In that time he had seen just about everything, or at least he thought he had. Until now. The vicious potential of the anonymous letter writer had escaped his attention to this point. Having accomplished much in his early service as dean, Adams had come to believe that long-term survival depended primarily on political strategy. With the added demands of fundraising in recent years, he placed ever more reliance on subordinates. He had scant patience with people who fell short. That scant patience quickly dropped to zero if the faculty got on the prod.

The dean understood where the real power was. The president, provost, and dean, even the board, won battles. The faculty won wars. Controversy was one thing. Adams actually enjoyed a good scrap now and then. Pitched battle was another. One needed to nip problems in the bud, something he had tried to explain to this fellow Wallace more than once. Much later, Adams would come to realize that telling someone they needed to do something in no way sufficed for explaining how. The how was the hard part.

The dean got Wallace situated in one of the upholstered chairs across his coffee table. "Who do you think sent this?" he asked, looking over the top of his glasses, letter in hand. "If I understand the situation right, it tends toward Marcus Jones's position, at least with regard to Rodriguez."

Wallace thought that too, but did not buy the idea that the hothead wrote it. "Jones always says what is on his mind, over and over," he said. "I can't see him thinking he has to resort to an anonymous letter." He paused, not wanting to sound paranoid, but went on with his own theory. "Actually, Del Baronne just might do something like this to stir the pot. He would know he could never be linked to it because it argues against him and his own position. I hope that doesn't sound paranoid."

"Well," Adams remarked, unable to resist a little black humor, "just because you're paranoid, doesn't mean they aren't out to get you. What do you think his motive would be?"

"I am completely clueless on that," Fred replied. "I cannot imagine how he could get a thing out of it. So from that standpoint, it must be someone else."

Adams was silent, thoughtfully looking at the ceiling, hands clasped behind his neck. He had his own theory about that, which he would keep to himself. Delbert Baronne had come to see him when the search for a new head started over a year ago. He had said he wanted to apply. He knew he could get the program on track. He had asked Adams if he would support him, or if there was any reason he should not be a candidate. Adams had said he felt they should look outside the department and that it might not be in Baronne's best interest to apply, at least at this time.

Actually, Adams had nothing against inside candidates. When the insider was someone he thought would be a team player and could get the job done, he would try to find a way to get them into the position. Baronne, being a long-time Adams observer, knew this. So he also would have deduced that the dean did not want him in the job. He would have been right for one simple reason: Adams did not trust him. And in the dead of night, standing alone in his den after his wife had gone to bed, with the music turned up loud, Adams might even have admitted that he was afraid of Baronne. The man would see this as a way to get rid of Wallace, put pressure on the dean, and get himself appointed in the vacuum that followed. Baronne had a controlling personality and a powerful ability to articulate an impeccable line of logic. Along with an extra edge of intelligence and information, some of which he manufactured himself, he had an uncanny ability to impose his views on most of his colleagues. A hothead like Jones provided Baronne with the perfect spark with which to light fires. He had others under his influence as well, whom he could call upon to throw gasoline as needed.

Of course, who wrote the letter was just speculation. More to the point, the dean could see that the Rodriguez issue must be separated from all the others. His advisory council, comprised of six tenured full professors, was split right down the middle on Rodriguez. The six included two women and one African American man. The dean's calculus said that these demographics would help him through a grievance, if one resulted, from the negative recommendation he intended to make. He also believed it likely that there would come a time, fairly soon, when Wallace would be leaving office.

Wallace was staring at him, obviously wondering what he was thinking. Abruptly, Adams summed up his position. "Look Fred," he said, "you are going to have to get this situation contained. First, you have got to be able to control faculty meetings. I get the sense they run themselves. Then, you have got to get the Rodriguez tenure case separated from all these other issues. Get these other items on a new agenda that does not include tenure, and get this thing in hand."

The two men began to head for the door, chitchatting about Christmas, family, and so forth. They touched very briefly on the Ph.D. program. Adams allowed as to how there was no way to forecast what the board ultimately would do with it. Shortly, Fred Wallace was on his way home. Thinking back on the meeting, he could not recall learning a thing that would really help him. Maybe he had a little clearer notion of what needed to happen, but no real idea how to go about it. He wished he could talk all this over with someone and try to get all the dots to connect. But he really did not know where to go with that.

On January 14, Wallace convened a meeting of the English department faculty. Everyone from instructor up was there. Neither tenure, promotion, nor anything related to it was up for discussion. The agenda included the following: preliminary enrollment projections, faculty teaching loads and class size, teaching assistant loads and class size, update on the budget (as per the last dean's cabinet meeting), clarification and update on the Ph.D. program. It included every item other than tenure that was causing tension in the department. By the time January 14 rolled around, Fred was almost looking forward to the meeting, which was to start at 3:00 p.m. and could run to 5:00 p.m. if need be.

Wallace passed the agenda around the room. After making a few introductory remarks about how several of the items were obviously related, for example, enrollment projections, the fiscal environment, and class size, he recited the central administration's most recent enrollment projections and extrapolated how those would affect enrollment in the upper- and lower-division classes in their department. No problem. He did notice a number of people were reading the agenda and he couldn't tell if they were listening to him. The item on faculty teaching loads and class size devoured 90 minutes of acrimonious venting and arguing.

After making several cynical observations early, in between Marcus Jones's spittle-sprinkled outbursts, Fred Baronne seized a pause in the debate to state, "Why couldn't we have received this agenda a week ago? We actually might have been able to accomplish something today if we could have had the enrollment data and the agenda at the end of last week."

Wallace squirmed. He had to acknowledge the truth in Baronne's assertion. He then suggested that now at least everyone had the information and knew what the issues were. That said, he went on to the teaching assistant load and class size item. At 5:30, after a blizzard of claims and counterclaims based on real and manufactured data, the meeting broke up with Baronne demanding that the graduate students and TAs have an opportunity to be heard at another meeting. At that point, Wallace snapped; just for a moment.

"Dammit, Baronne," he barked. "Let's get one thing straight. You are not the head of this department." He stopped, knowing this was a mistake, but charged ahead anyway. "Your ideas are welcome, but your never-ending attempts to control this program are not. We have other smart people here, who need to get a word in edgewise once in a while. This meeting is over." And with that he left the room, slamming the door so hard he cracked the old, pebbled glass. Some would say he "stormed out in a huff." Faculty members sat dumbfounded, then began to trickle out a few at a time. The implications of their deteriorating situation were beginning sink in. They never had made it to the Ph.D. item.

Thenceforth, events unfolded precipitously. The first faculty senate session of the semester took place three days following the English department's meeting. During the open comment item, Trenton Bartlett asked to be recognized and stood to declare that although he did not like to talk about specific situations, given that the senate should stick to policy matters and all, he knew that some senators had received copies of an anonymous letter decrying conditions in the English department. He, of course, like his colleagues, had little use for anonymous letters. However, when things got bad enough and fear of retribution began to affect even tenured faculty members, one could not dismiss the warning signs. Majors in every program depended on a stable English department because every single undergraduate student was required to take basic courses there. They all had a stake in this. The fiduciary obligations of the senate demanded that steps be taken to ensure that the situation was brought to hand. Without claiming to make judgment, Bartlett asserted that leadership had broken down. The head seemed to be letting matters run out of control and had been reported to have behaved in a churlish, even aggressive manner against one faculty member who was attempting to lend a hand in getting the department's affairs on track.

Crumm and his colleagues met with the president and provost to urge their engagement in the issues affecting the English department. While both had some awareness of them, neither realized the level to which the situation seemed to have escalated, even after the anonymous letter. Crumm himself had not swallowed the story whole, but felt obligated to ensure that the administration knew a serious problem was afoot and that it was under examination.

The provost took the matter up with the dean. Adams was taken aback that affairs had gotten out from under him so quickly. He had intended to alert the provost, but been beaten to the punch, so he looked bad. He allowed as how he had reservations about Wallace but was hoping he could get him and his department on a better trajectory.

Rodriguez's tenure and promotion were denied. The logic was that a majority of the department faculty, the department head, and the dean all had recommended against tenure, and the dean's advisory committee was split. A grievance resulted. Wallace looked especially bad in the grievance hearing. It came to light that distracted by his other problems, he initially had not included Rodriguez's letters of reference in his tenure packet but had distributed them to the voting faculty members only after they met to discuss the case. If either the dean or the provost had caught this, they could have sent the matter back for reconsideration. It gave the hearing panel a reason to recommend Rodriguez's tenure and promotion. They wanted to do so anyway because they had the uneasy feeling he had not been treated fairly. The president supported their recommendation. Because Wallace looked bad, Adams did also. Ditto for the provost.

Dean Adams had two meetings with the faculty of the English department, one with Fred Wallace present and one with him absent. He also had several discussions with the provost. The upshot of it was that Wallace stepped down at the end of the semester. Delbert Baronne got the surprise of his life. Janice Fillmore was named acting head, and she did so well that she wound up with the regular appointment. Fillmore managed to neutralize Baronne and Jones completely. Fortunately, when it got down to naming an interim head, the dean had the sense to meet with each member of the faculty individually to obtain their views. Janice clearly had strong support, with one reservation—could she stand up to the aggressive forces that came from some quarters in the department?

She could and did. Her primary strategy was to empower everyone else. She had a clear agenda for each department meeting, which was distributed at least two days ahead of time. She invited the dean to a department meeting twice the first fall and at least once a semester thereafter to be certain he knew where the department was headed and whether he approved or disapproved. When a new item was discussed during meetings, she went around the table and had every individual render comments. She met with every faculty member at least once a semester in addition to the annual goal setting and evaluation meeting.

These discussions achieved a level of coherence sufficient to allow the faculty to reach a consensus on some very basic issues. Central to this was the future direction and priorities of the department. It was very tough going, but they finally reached something resembling consensus and let the Ph.D. degree go. They also began a long-term effort to build more strength in a smaller number of specialties.

Fillmore saw that Baronne had certain talents that were best channeled in specific directions. She formally designated him as coordinator of the undergraduate program.

Fred Wallace became a very productive faculty member. He took the department up a level in his field. Realizing that he was not really cut out for administration, he took the high road in supporting his successor.

Hector Rodriguez never felt entirely comfortable in the department, although he was very productive and Janice Fillmore worked mightily to put him at ease. Within two years, he accepted an offer at another university. This was a serious loss in many ways for the cultural perspective of the department, college, and university.

DISCUSSION

This example case has many issues going on simultaneously, and sometimes it is difficult to make sense them. That is one of the points. When conflict gets out of hand and affects an entire unit, a number of issues are in play; they are multifaceted and complicated by inadequate information. Add to that mix an array of complicated personalities, one or more of which might not want resolution, and the conflict can escalate very rapidly.

Fred Wallace was hired because of prominence in his specialty. This was important, of course, and the fact that he had no prior administrative experience should not have disqualified him. However, he was immediately baptized by immersion—in fire. If he had had an opportunity for a honeymoon period, or a year of routine activity to learn the job on his own, he might have been successful. However, he encountered serious problems starting on day one. Obviously, there was no structured training or orientation program in place. In normal circumstances, an effective mentoring program might have compensated for this shortcoming. In the absence of a designated mentor (e.g., an experienced head from another department), the obvious person to do this was the dean. Although he met with the dean on occasion to discuss the issues in his department, he received little wisdom or real help in dealing with them. The dean tended to be long on telling Wallace what to do and short on coaching him on how to go about it.

Unfortunately, the dean was preoccupied with his own interests. Clearly he had made a positive impact in his early years of service. However, having reached a certain plateau, he had begun to concentrate more on political survival. Worse yet, the course of events suggests that he had become willing to use others, in this case Wallace and, for that matter, Rodriguez, as foils in order to protect himself. Everyone paid a price for this in terms of mental and emotional stress and strain, lost productivity, and programmatic stagnation.

With some instinct for the job and coaching from the dean, Wallace could have headed off many of his problems early. He would have been aided greatly in this effort by some degree of leadership from a critical mass of senior faculty. If he had moved decisively in the first two or three weeks to do the things Janice Fillmore subsequently did, he might have averted the worst of his problems.

Janice Fillmore was far tougher and smarter than anyone realized. Her good instinct, intelligence, common sense, and ability to handle stress were complemented by two other pluses. First, she had an opportunity to observe the problems and adverse dynamics, and she took advantage of it. Second, by the time she was appointed, her colleagues fully realized how serious their problems had become. They had looked into the abyss and seen how far they could fall. They realized that if the situation was not turned around, everyone's career would suffer, students would be disenfranchised, and they would be miserable individually and collectively for an interminable period. She capitalized on this by creating a format and atmosphere that empowered everyone. This diluted Jones's opportunities for temper outbursts and Baronne's for connivances to the point that they were minimized, if not altogether neutralized. She also realized, perhaps intuitively, that she could not place full reliance on the dean to support her. By inviting him to departmental faculty meetings at key points, she literally co-opted him into being her ally.

One may also suspect, although it is not explicit in the narrative, that the provost had taken his hands off the wheel. He should have been getting wind of the controversy and asking the dean what he knew about it long before the anonymous letter, and certainly before the faculty senate leadership came to see him and the president.

It is evident that Upper Valley University had no organized, well-understood, readily accessible support system for conflict resolution. Also, consider what a difference it would have made if Fred Wallace had a thorough orientation on department-level administration very early in his service as department head. If he had been able to meet regularly with others in similar positions to exchange experience and ideas, it would have helped in terms of learning the job and gaining moral support. If he could have called upon real expertise in addressing adversarial patterns of behavior it would have been a blessing. Some basic training in things as simple as how to run an effective meeting would have worked wonders. Such support would not only have helped Fred, it would have saved the taxpayers a lot of money and the faculty and students a lot of misery.

Appendix 3: An Instance of Gender Bias

Max Anderson was standing outside the back door of Lee Town Middle School, smoking a cigarette while commiserating with Eldon Sharp. They both taught seventh grade. Some days Max was ready to hang up teaching and go to work for his brother-in-law selling annuities. Teaching had become a combination of social worker, probation officer, and instructor. At times he felt more like a babysitter than the teacher he had set out to be. Too often, he was the heavy because the parents (or, more frequently, parent) wanted to be the child's friend instead of his parent.

Max blew out a cloud of smoke, whipped away by the cold wind. "That Whitaker kid," he allowed, "is a mean little twerp."

"He can be," Eldon replied, looking at his watch and snubbing out his smoke. "But I don't think he's really a bad kid. He can be funny as hell. And he is very, very smart. He takes to math like a duck to water. Sometimes, I think one reason he gets into so much trouble is that he's just bored stiff. What's he done this time?"

"Poked Sally Aarons in the back with a pencil. Broke the lead off under the skin."

"Hmm, not good."

"His mom's an angel," Max said, holding the door open as they went back to work. "She seems to hang in there with him, but she sure has her hands full."

Laura Whitaker was 37. Her son Sean was 13. She had been divorced for four years. No need to go into the details, but it was a long, complicated story. She and Wes had been hired at Western Ridge College as a dual-career deal. They both had been young, aspiring assistant professors at the time. Laura was on the software side of database management in the computing science department in arts and sciences, and Wes was an information management whiz in the management department of the business school. Their careers seemed to be a perfect match that ought to have brought synergy to their marriage. Between the two of them, they made very good money, especially with a little consulting thrown in. Sean liked grade school and did well in it. How could things get better? They didn't. They got worse. Much worse.

Even with the ferocious efficiency of the rumor mill at Western, Laura seemed to be the last person alive to figure out that Wes was seeing an assistant professor in the accounting department on the side. The whole thing turned very nasty. About the same time Laura found out about it, the gossip circuit exploded into the open. Within days of Laura and Wes telling him they were getting a divorce, Sean heard it at school, complete with details. Within months, Wes and his new significant other had moved to Nevada. The Las Vegas metro area was in the throes of a population explosion and demand was high. Wes was still in the field of information management and doing well, with all the necessary qualifiers thrown in. The "other" was teaching accounting in a nearby community college. They had long since split.

With four years under her belt as a divorcee and single mom, Laura was still learning the harsh realities of raising what had become a rebellious teenager and keeping a career on track. This was all the more challenging in a discipline that changed and added content with explosive speed. Laura had been tenured and promoted to associate professor three years ago. She had generated enough momentum in her first five years as assistant professor that she was able to sleepwalk through the sixth year and her divorce at the same time. She desperately wanted to be a full professor in two more years.

Now, with her fourth year as an associate professor under way, Laura was having an early fall talk with Farley Johnson, chair of the

Department of Computing Science. She was pushing herself toward promotion to full professor, and she wanted to be sure Farley was with her. Her personal pride and sense of accomplishment were strong motivators. She had a real passion for her work and a relentless curiosity that drove her scholarship. Laura was very good at integrating her research into her teaching. She understood the synergy that comes from good students asking tough questions. She had to maintain momentum. Loss of momentum at this stage of her career could be very hard to overcome, and she was going to need all the earning power she could generate in the future.

Without doubt, she had been treading water the last couple of years. Laura knew that all too well. She had a real head of steam built up going into the tenure and promotion decision, but that was playing out, as one problem followed another during and after the divorce, most recently with Sean. At first she had thought he was going to sail through the breakup in one piece. No such luck. Her son's plane trip to Vegas for the obligatory first visit with his dad seemed to jar him off course. He had yet to get his bearings. Farley had been a champ about the whole thing, finding every way he could to increase her flexibility. Her colleagues had been very understanding. Chester Romaine had picked up a course for her, mid-semester, for almost a month when Sean got into a vandalism scrape and had a couple of other brushes with the law and the school administration. Laura worked more at home, mainly to be there when school was out. Farley had helped with her teaching schedule, and she had a system going that worked, up to a point. All of these compensatory arrangements had cut into her interaction with collaborators. She had lost a graduate student because she was hard to contact in person. She still had one major grant. She and Farley needed to discuss what it was going to take for her to generate a renewal and get new proposals out the door. This required critical mass that Laura could not generate alone, although she knew she could be a very strong member, or leader, of a collaborative team. But teams were getting harder to build.

Farley Johnson had been department chair for 12 years, a long time by Western Ridge standards. The department had progressed far under his leadership. People liked and trusted him. Farley was a large man, with a big, square face. He had a massive grin with a gap between his two front teeth that reminded Laura of C sharp on a baby grand. Farley moved the day-to-day work of the department on time, and he had an uncanny sense of where computing was going and where the niches were that his department might fill. He had a knack for finding money, private, university, and federal. He worked hard at coaching young faculty, whether in teaching or in getting research ideas funded and high-quality papers published. The net effect of Farley's work was that he helped build careers and strengthened the department in one synergistic flow of intellectual energy. That was to the good of all. However, at the end of the current academic year, Farley was stepping down. At 62, he wanted to finish his two doctoral students, wrap up the one grant he still had, get the papers out, and then maybe teach part-time. He even considered retiring altogether in a couple of years.

Farley had a little round table with three chairs in front of the one window in his office. He would like to have had four, but there wasn't room. At one time, he had the table in a corner on the other side of the office. Back then he did have four chairs around it, but he always felt the person in the corner looked trapped. Sometimes he thought they felt trapped as well. The window worked better. The light was good and the view from the second story was nice. Attendees at Farley's little tabletop conferences could see one end of the pond in front of McGarrity Hall and scores of students hustling by at every class change. With the window open, you could hear them talking. Bobbing hair, laughter, and gossip about professors, love affairs, and sports, all jumbled together as part of the campus scene he loved.

Farley always sat in the east chair, even when the sun was in his eyes. The reason was simple. His wife Irene had once given him a little pewter clock, about two inches square. Farley kept it on a bookshelf behind the west chair, tucked into the lee of a lacquered wooden bowl he had picked up at the GUM store in Moscow. He could glance up at the little clock without anyone noticing. Usually this was to check on the time without looking at his watch, which he viewed to be rude to his guests. Lately, though, he often looked up at the little clock because it reminded him of Irene.

About a year ago, Irene had lost a 10-year battle with breast cancer. Funny how many different ways he missed her. Had she been there, he might very well have discussed Laura Whitaker's situation with her when he went home that evening. It was always good to think out loud with her about problems of most any kind. Irene had possessed an intuitive common sense that seemed to raise the right questions. Farley missed that, just like he would miss helping his faculty pursue their aspirations, solve their professional problems, and sometimes their personal ones as well. Running his hand through his thinning hair, Farley fell to kneading his right ear lobe between his forefinger and thumb and regarded Laura Whitaker, sitting across his table nursing a cup of his favorite green tea.

This was one very sharp woman, in Farley Johnson's assessment. She had come far, to this point, in a field dominated by men. Some would assert, and rightly so in his view, that computing had a protracted history of bias against women. Of course, some believed otherwise and would deny it to the last breath. He knew personally more than one female computing scientist who published under her initials rather than her given name. The data on publication rates supported this strategy. The level of Laura's work had been such that she had prospered in this male-dominated environment. She had brought in some very competitive grants and published ten papers, individually and as a second or third author, in very strong journals.

Not exactly pretty, Laura Whitaker was striking and made the most of it. She had fine features with brown eyes and brown hair beginning to show a little gray around the temples. She usually pulled it back, but today it was down, almost shoulder length. Laura's hands were very expressive. She tended to have her forearms and hands on the tabletop, palms up or palms down, and to gesture in subtle ways. Right now, she had her right hand on page six of her resume, stroking it back and forth as if to polish up the contents.

"Farley," Laura said, "you and I both know I have not hit my usual pace the last couple of years. But it's not exactly like I've been standing still. I had one Ph.D. finish last spring and another will finish this December. I have the Department of Education grant and two proposals out. My student ratings are excellent. You even use me as an example now and again. So, my publications have tailed off some. I've had a lot to absorb. Given what I've been dealing with, my productivity is relatively high. It really is."

For Laura, this was a long speech. She tended to be sparse with the rhetoric and very much on point. Farley mostly agreed with her self-assessment, but not entirely.

"Given everything you have had going on," he responded, rubbing the muscle along his right jaw, "I agree. You have stayed in the game. There are some important questions to think about, though. As an associate professor, you stack up very well in this department. But are you ready for promotion to full professor, given the level the department is at now versus 10 years ago? Will the faculty support you? Some would say it is early, although that shouldn't be an issue. But do you have a big enough, solid enough body of work now to be a full professor in this department? I have to be straight with you, Laura, I don't think you are there yet."

He knew that wasn't what Laura wanted to hear, but he could see she was not surprised, either. "Look, Farley," she said, "you have been great for this department and good for me. You have helped me get through a very hard time and keep my career on track. But I am in a bind here. You and I both have seen people in situations like this spend the rest of their career as a frustrated associate professor."

Laura Whitaker went on to explain what they both already understood at some level. If Farley was going to continue as chair, they could develop goals and strategy she could follow over the next couple of years and be promoted. But with a new chair coming in, or being appointed from the faculty, that would become very difficult. True, the senior faculty would still be there for the most part, and they would provide some continuity in values and standards. But a new chair would have an impact. It also was the case that the dean had been in office for just two years, and she was starting to move the college in a more research-oriented direction, with emphasis on competitive funding. The standards would change. They had in the past.

"Look," Farley replied, "we know you are in a solid, rapidly developing specialty. It will continue to be a departmental priority. Let's develop the best strategy we can, then you can go over it with the new chair as soon as one is designated."

And that is exactly what they did. One goal was to prevent any slippage in Laura's teaching effectiveness and build on it where possible. Another was to get two additional proposals developed and in the mail. Specific timelines would mesh with granting agency deadlines and funding dates that would allow the projects to be under way no later than 18 months hence. Other goals included adding two new doctoral students and getting four to six key publications in press or print over a two-year period. The grant proposals would demand at least two co-principal investigators, one of whom would be in the computing science department, the other from Industrial Engineering. Farley would be her advocate.

Laura left on firmer footing. After walking what seemed like five miles to the north parking lot, she aimed her Camry for Sean's school. She was very distressed about the scheduled meeting with the principal regarding this bizarre incident in which her son had been accused of stabbing a girl in the back with a pencil. It had become clear that there was more to it than that, but it had shaken her to the core. As she pulled off campus into the flow of traffic, she heard a siren and saw an ambulance screaming down on her. She would learn later that it was making a fruitless siren run to the building she had just left. While Laura was walking from Elgin Hall to the north lot, Farley Johnson was on the floor of his office, dying of a ruptured aneurysm in his brain.

One year later, Laura Whitaker was sitting in a director's chair on her screened-in porch. She was sipping a glass of Pinot Grigio and solving the world's problems with Maria Grafton. Sean was in his room, surfing every web site he could find on Egyptian archeology in preparation for a school paper. Specifically, he had become caught up in the controversy between a group of geologists and traditional Egyptologists about the age of the Sphinx. Maria was an associate professor in high-energy physics. Like computing science, physics had a history of being a hard row to hoe for women, although there were some success stories.

To some extent, the tide was beginning to turn in both fields. This was due in no small part to the aftermath of the gender bias controversy at the Massachusetts Institute of Technology. Laura and Maria had a lot in common career-wise, but that was about it. As different as they were as individuals, though, the two women hit it off.

Laura Whitaker was still affected by Farley Johnson's death, both personally and professionally. She was frustrated with the new chair and some of her other colleagues as well. This had a great deal to do with how some of the faculty, one in particular, viewed her work and her personally. Laura was getting angry. She was not, however, mad at the world, nor did she harbor a generic anger about men.

She was feeling better about Sean. In fact, on some days Laura felt great about him. She had paid a price, to be sure, in blood, sweat, tears, time and, to some extent, money, getting him to this point without her job falling apart. She had managed to accomplish a lot with both her son and her work.

In some ways, Maria Grafton was in a similar situation with her career. A six-year associate professor, she was doing well in an extremely competitive department. Sometimes the competition became very fierce, indeed. But then in big science you lived and died by the grant dollar. If you were a lousy teacher, you would not make it, period. But if you were a mediocre to good teacher, then that was the baseline and you gained or lost on your research. Fair enough. That kind of aggressive drive was one of the ingredients for getting a man on the moon, finding up and down quarks, making heart valve replacement a reality, and thousands of other advances in mankind's lot. The issue with Maria was that if you didn't get fair distribution of lab space, course assignment, and a clear shot at the best graduate students, the playing field was uneven at best. She felt there was a general tendency for women to get the short end of the stick in all those areas.

Maria had been married and divorced in less than two years, back in graduate school days. Thankfully, there had been no children. The whole thing had been painful but quick. It was soon in the past. She had found that kind of relationship was not what she wanted. She also found out that men could be pretty bad. Her mother had been right, she had decided, in her oft-expressed wisdom that men were generally a sorry lot, her father being a classic example. Just under the surface, sometimes close enough to be obvious, Maria was angry.

Maria was a brilliant woman. She could be a lot of fun. On good days, she had a great wit, dry and salty. Laura found her to be a good sounding board because she was a scientist, and a woman. There weren't all that many to turn to for conversation about your career. When she got in a bind with Sean, though, Maria was not a source of help. Laura had finally found a good child psychologist who really was effective, but she supplemented the doctor's services with healthy doses of consultation with her parents. She had found that the unsettling effects of Sean's visits to his dad and his seemingly infinite variety of female companions was best offset by lengthy visits to her parent's home in Maine. A month of fishing with his grandpa, eating his grandmother's incredible cooking, and absorbing little snippets of subtle wisdom was a superior way to get a teenager's head back on straight.

"The thing is, Laura," Maria was saying, "these people just don't know what to do with women. Most want to keep us on the fringe to fulfill the token woman role, and the ones that want to get us in the game are half afraid of us. Why, I'm not sure."

Laura thought the term *these people* cast too big a net around an ill-defined space. "There's no mystery there," she replied, "some of them, mainly the ones who might want to work with us, are scared to death they will say or do the wrong thing and we will slap an affirmative action complaint on them—or worse."

"And maybe we should." Maria made a swipe through the bean dip with a baked tortilla crisp and topped off her wine glass. "This is a generic problem," she continued. "It's systemic in every university and this one is no exception. And every man is part of it—the evildoers themselves, and the ones who won't do anything about it."

"I don't buy that, Maria, I just don't." Laura was clearly agitated. "Take Farley Johnson as an example. Farley did more for my career than any other single person, ever, man or woman. I owe him. You can't just paint all men with the same brush. Some really do help. Far-

ley, God bless him, was one. Others would like to and just don't know
how to go about it. You're right, though, that there are some out there
who just don't think we ought to be in their game and actively try to
undermine us. We both could name a few."

"OK, so let's assume there is some truth in all that," Maria said.
"Now take the treatment you get from that irreparable nincompoop,
Mason Hammond. He's a full professor, although only God knows
how, and he should be helping. Instead, he opposes you every time
you need something from the department. You know for a fact that he
actively leaned on at least three top Ph.D. candidates to get them to
choose other major professors. At least two of them would have gone to
you." She paused for bean dip and a deep breath. "Now how is it that
what's his name, Johnson's replacement, doesn't get him in line and
support you? That's a fair question, is it not?"

That, Laura knew, was the heart of the problem. Farley Johnson
had been a genius at quietly neutralizing the likes of Hammond and,
a time or two, had really jerked his chain. Farley's successor, Darryl
Halstead, had been appointed as acting chair when Farley died. He got
on pretty well and most people supported him. The dean had wanted
to go outside and use Farley's position to bring in a new chair. Most of
the faculty fought that strategy tooth and nail. They had pushed for using the salary to hire a new assistant professor, with what was left over
going into salary enhancements for existing faculty. The dean finally
figured she had other battles that were more important at the moment and gave in, but not all the way. The salary enhancements, about
$20,000 in all, were distributed on the six associate and full professors
with the highest average annual evaluation over the past three years.
Laura had missed out on that by a hair. Indirectly, that did not help
her push for promotion. It was also the case, though, that she had supported the dean as aggressively as she could to bring in a new chair with
a national search. She believed it could have been a great opportunity
to strengthen the department. Mason Hammond had fought it like
Horatio at the bridge, and he had been left gasping when the dean distributed the money personally, before she appointed Darryl Halstead.

Hammond was not among the six recipients. Productivity definitely had conquered politics in that instance.

"Let's keep in mind," Laura pointed out, "that we have a woman dean now. You and I are both in her college. She strikes me as a very tough cookie."

"All right," Maria asked, "suppose you go to see the dean, which is an eminently good idea. You have some really tangible things to complain about. Just what would you say?"

Laura thought about that long and hard for several days. She was able to clarify the issues as she saw them. As a result, she settled on a game plan.

She would talk to Darryl Halstead first because she did not want to burn bridges unnecessarily. Also, there was a remote possibility that he would actually do something. Her points at issue were that the transition from Johnson to Halstead had changed the dynamics for the plan, and even the possibilities, she and Farley had agreed to; Mason Hammond was exhibiting visible, personal antagonism toward her, including actions that were thwarting her opportunities; Darryl Halstead pretended to be unaware of it, declined to believe it, and refused to do anything about it. As proof of her position, she had firsthand accounts from more than one of her colleagues that Hammond worked behind the scenes to undermine the value of her work and to discourage others from collaborating with her. He specifically had urged three graduate students not to choose Laura as their major professor. One, reportedly, would say so.

The one issue about which she remained undecided was whether to attribute all or part of her dilemma to bias based on her gender. In her own mind, that clearly was the case, but she did not want to be viewed for the rest of her career at Western as a woman who became a full professor because of an affirmative action dispute. She knew she deserved promotion on the merits. In the end, she decided to hold off on that, even though Maria and two or three other female colleagues were urging her to go whole hog and file a discrimination complaint against Hammond and possibly Halstead as well.

"And while you're at it," Maria had asserted, "throw a sexual harassment complaint against that arrogant, condescending S.O.B. Mason Hammond. Some of the things he has said about you cannot go unaddressed. You would have a lot of support, I guarantee it."

By this, Maria was referring primarily to remarks Hammond allegedly made to a graduate student and another full professor to the effect that "Dr. Whitaker is smart enough and has some good ideas, but she is so bogged down in her personal life that she relies on being a woman to get ahead. It's not this department's responsibility to compensate for her having a problem child at home." Or words to that effect.

He was also alleged to have said in a social setting off campus that he wished someone could help Laura Whitaker get her life in order. If she would rely on her science instead of invoking sympathy as a beleaguered single mother, she could advance her career and make a difference in the department. Or words to that effect.

Laura determined to see the matter through, at least for now, on the merits of her work and provable patterns of behavior affecting it, without making direct reference to her gender.

A few days later, Laura met with Darryl Halstead and had a very candid conversation. At least she was candid. She never could be quite sure about Halstead. Her comments were predicated, as she said to her chair, on the understanding that she also was going to have the same discussion with the dean. Halstead was defensive about that, urging her to give him a chance to deal with her concerns. Laura responded that this was not a new development and too much time had been lost already. She then proceeded to enumerate the key points, including the fact that he, Halstead, was unable or unwilling to provide any support. Her purpose here was to do him the courtesy of knowing everything she intended to say to the dean. She had held these concerns for months, indeed since soon after Farley Johnson died. She had discussed them with Halstead on more than one occasion, and nothing had happened. He could work to resolve these issues in parallel with her going to see the dean, but she was waiting no longer. Thus, Laura Whitaker came to have a meeting with the dean of arts and sciences, Willa Schlesinger.

Dean Schlesinger was not from the sciences, but she had a real grasp of the issues pertaining to them, including those of race and gender. The biggest issue, of course, was that there were far too few women in the basic sciences, and the number of people of color was small. This included mathematics. Schlesinger herself was a speech therapist. She had served in one capacity or another in three universities and had, for a short time, been an assistant deputy Secretary of Education.

The dean did not subscribe to the traditional power dressing modality adopted by some women in similar roles. The dark suit and silk scarf under the chin were not for her. She leaned more toward dresses, slacks, pantsuits, blouses, and jewelry. Sparse with makeup, she used it to advantage, especially around her eyes. Subtle and gray, Willa Schlesinger's eyes were expressive and penetrating. They created the perception that she missed nothing. That perception would reflect reality. A keen observer and student of people's motives, the dean was careful about understanding situations before committing herself to a position or making a decision. Soft spoken, she sometimes gave the impression that she could be pushed around. In her short tenure in office, several unfortunates had made the mistake of trying. Without ever raising her voice or being disrespectful, she had cut a couple of people off at the knees in situations that left a lasting impression across the college. She was smart, fair, and good to work with, but not to be taken lightly. And, she clearly had the full, if not unquestioning, support of the provost.

Laura Whitaker gave the dean what she considered to be the full relevant background on her situation, including the general framework of her personal life, the impact it had on her work, and the steps she had taken to overcome it. She gave Schlesinger a copy of her current resume and a detailed description of recent accomplishments. She did not mince words in describing Mason Hammond's attitude and behavior, the effect he seemed to have in influencing several faculty and graduate students, and Darryl Halstead's lack of effectiveness.

The dean had been around the block many times. After asking a number of questions about the factual basis of Laura's assertions, not all of which could be verified immediately, she went directly to the point Whitaker had decided to leave out.

"You are," she observed, "the only tenured woman in your department. Yet you have specifically not mentioned gender as an issue. So let me be direct. Do you believe these circumstances you have described result in any significant way from the fact that you are a woman in a discipline that has some history about gender equity?"

Put that way, coming from the dean, Laura was forced to rapidly rethink her own perceptions about discrimination because that was exactly what Schlesinger was asking about. Over the next few minutes, she was able to clarify her thinking on this at a level she had not achieved previously. As her thoughts developed, it became clear that she could attribute different motives to different individuals in the department.

In her view, Professor Hammond was clearly influenced, along with whatever other factors, by her gender. She felt this was substantiated by remarks he had made, some in her presence and some reported to her, about her personal life, her son, and her alleged reliance on her gender for advancement of her career. She felt the graduate students were simply being bullied into taking the actions they had, and the same was true of one and maybe two young assistant professors that were potential collaborators in her specialty. She viewed Halstead as simply lacking the fortitude to assume his responsibilities.

The dean did not swallow Laura's story with one gulp. However, she saw issues of importance embedded in it that must be addressed. She also had some points of clarification that would become crucial in eventually resolving the problems that Laura and her department faced. One of these was that, if true, and she suspected it was, Laura's concerns confirmed her initial misgivings about appointing Darryl Halstead as chair of computing science. Whether his performance could be improved by some intensive professional development and better mentoring on her part remained to be determined. She did not divulge that aspect of her assessment to Laura Whitaker. What she did share was an initial reframing of the issues as she saw them.

First, Dean Schlesinger opined, while doltish and inappropriate, remarks allegedly made by Professor Hammond in a social setting off campus, although possibly providing context, could not be influential in determining discrimination, at least from the university's perspective. Remarks he allegedly made to graduate students and faculty might, to the extent they could be validated. If it could be verified that Hammond had pressured graduate students to avoid Laura as a major professor, for reasons that related to her gender or family and personal circumstances, then the implications would be serious, in her view, and might support a claim of discrimination within the context of other statements the man allegedly had made.

As their discussion had eventually revealed, Laura believed that Professor Hammond had taken specific actions and said specific damaging things that were influenced by, or based upon, Dr. Whitaker's gender. This constituted a claim of gender discrimination. The university had specific policies on that issue that every administrative officer was obligated to follow. Specifically, the matter could not be ignored. Pursuing it to a conclusion must involve consultation with the Office of Affirmative Action. Toward that end, the dean committed to collect Professor Halstead and meet with an affirmative action officer to determine whether, if true, Hammond's behavior would constitute discrimination or sexual harassment. If so, the complaint would be handled by the affirmative action office. If not, the dean would initiate a process, yet to be determined, to get to the bottom of the matter.

Finally, the dean established that Professor Whitaker's assessment of Dr. Halstead's performance in failing to address her concerns was an administrative performance issue. She had appointed Halstead. He reported to her and served at her pleasure. She would take responsibility for addressing those matters administratively.

On the assumption that the dean would follow through, Laura Whitaker was pleasantly surprised at how far the meeting with her had gone. She was somewhat taken aback at Schlesinger's direct, precise approach and nervous about the discrimination aspect.

The dean did follow through. She recognized the impact of timing and that this was the moment to get emerging problems in the computing science department nipped in the bud. She immediately initiated the meeting between herself, Darryl Halstead, and an affirmative action officer. Parallel to that, she asked Dr. Halstead for his side of Professor Whitaker's concern that he had ignored her complaint. The gist of his response was that he did not want Whitaker's issues to become divisive in the department. He had tried to encourage her to just keep on toward the goals she and Farley Johnson had developed, and he would support that. When the dean asked about the possibility, even the likelihood, that one or more members of the faculty had worked to undermine those goals, he responded that he had heard rumors to that effect. When she asked if he had looked into those rumors, he said he thought that would be interpreted as a witch-hunt, and he feared that it would have a divisive effect. Mentally, the dean threw up her hands. She indicated to Halstead that they would return to these issues once the affirmative action consultation was concluded.

The affirmative action officer viewed the allegations about Professor Hammond's behavior to be serious, if true. His logic was that if Hammond had made remarks to or about Laura Whitaker's family issues and gender, within the context of the workplace, and those remarks were related to actions that had an impact on her ability to conduct her work and thus impede her career, they would meet the standards for discrimination. In keeping with university policy, the affirmative action officer and the dean conducted an organized but discreet review. The first step was to obtain a response from Professor Hammond to Laura Whitaker's assertions. He denied some components and agreed with others. On points where the facts were agreed upon, he presented a different perspective. The three graduate students were interviewed as well. One quoted Hammond as having said to him, "Dr. Whitaker is a very bright woman. She has done some good work. Unfortunately, she seems to have a lot of single mom issues that tie up her time. If it weren't for the fact that she is a woman, she would not, in his opinion, have been tenured. Farley Johnson had been her keeper, so to speak, and without him, she seemed to lack direction. It just might be better for your career if you looked at other faculty members for a major professor."

When asked if he had sought Hammond's opinion, or if Hammond had offered it spontaneously, the student indicated he had gone to Professor Hammond and asked his advice. Looking back on it, though, he thought he would have been better off going with Dr. Whitaker, as he had originally intended.

Two assistant professors were interviewed because Laura Whitaker had attempted to collaborate with them on grant proposals, and they had declined. Both said they had been reluctant to commit their time to working with her because "the word was" that she did not follow through, get the work done on time, and get the papers out the door. When asked where they got that impression, one identified two different faculty members and another identified Mason Hammond. When asked if they had ever seen Laura Whitaker's resume both said no.

When asked, as part of the review, what his observations and his role had been, Halstead said the same things he had told the dean in the first place.

The gray zone was too big for the case to meet the legal standard for discrimination or sexual harassment per se. At the same time, it was clear that the work atmosphere for Laura Whitaker was not appropriate and had been adversely impacted by Professor Hammond's actions, however well or ill intended they might have been. Halstead's inattention to the situation was criticized specifically. In addition to stating these observations, the final draft of the investigative finding stated that the dean would work with the chair and faculty of the department to get a number of important issues on the table. These would include the need to have a collective and collaborative approach to the department's work, to use all faculty resources to the best advantage in supporting graduate students and developing stronger research programs, and to develop a new strategic plan that would set forth the department's priorities for the next five to seven years. The dean saw to it that the last point was included because it needed to be done, and it would provide a constructive framework within which to address the other issues.

Parallel to the pursuit of these objectives, the dean would have a candid conversation with Professor Hammond. During it, she pointed out how close he was to serious trouble. And although the legal standard for discrimination or sexual harassment had not been met, he should be aware that there was reason to believe he had contributed to inappropriate setbacks in Laura Whitaker's career. Hammond did a credible job of explaining, as he had during the review, that he truly believed that Laura had been given preferential treatment because of her gender when Farley Johnson was chair. His further view was that she had been slacking off for two or three years due to family problems and was trying to get promoted in spite of it.

When asked by the dean if he thought Dr. Whitaker had proven talent, Hammond stated that she did. He went on to say that if she would just put it back to work, he could support her. When the dean asked him if he thought certain aspects of the atmosphere in the department were undermining her ability to do that, including his own attitude, Hammond paused for some while and said he would have to think that one through some more. However, Mason was astute enough to see which direction the wind was blowing. When asked by the dean if, while he was doing his thinking, he could play a positive role in the new efforts she was setting before the department, including collaborative mentoring among faculty, he said he would work whole heartedly to do just that.

That left one large loose end. The dean's plans for the department to right itself, and even take it up a notch, would take significant leadership and know-how in engaging all faculty members. In her view, although he might mature into the role at some point, Halstead was not up to the task. She had been looking into the services of a consultant the university was making available who might be a real asset. Justin Phillips had a Ph.D. in psychology and conducted a clinical practice in the community. He was not a university employee and had neither history nor clout within the institution. He had done some work with the Chamber of Commerce in strategic planning, including the facilitation of a recent retreat. Schlesinger interviewed him at length herself and discussed his track record with the provost, who gave him good marks. She came to the conclusion that with Phillips facilitating the problem solving and planning process, Halstead could stay in place, at least for the immediate future. She would engage Phillips to work with her, as a parallel project, to coach Halstead and make an honest effort to help him succeed.

Long term, the effort to get the department stabilized and to take it up a level was successful. The administrative development of Halstead, in the strict sense, was not. In the end, he made this decision himself and felt good about it. After his second year, he could see his scholarship going into the tank, and he really did not enjoy his work as chair. He yearned to plunge once again into full-time teaching and his own research in data security. He had not been accepting offers to consult with a number of firms because of time constraints. In fact, he could make more money without his administrative stipend, once he got back into doing some consulting. This time, the dean did conduct a national search for a new chair and hit a winner. A majority of the faculty saw the value in doing so. Mason Hammond expressed opposition initially, but only in a private meeting with the dean. When the decision was made, he supported it. Laura Whitaker became a full professor, but it took three years from the time of her complaint. She nailed down a clear niche in her specialty and had a body of work that withstood the closest scrutiny. People no longer thought about her affirmative action complaint except Mason Hammond on rare occasions, and he had pretty much put it behind him. This began one day when, at the end of a long, rocky meeting on collaboration, graduate student assignment, and other thorny issues, Justin Phillips fell in beside him. "You know, Mason," he said in an offhand way, "the future is a lot more fun when we stop dwelling on the past."

DISCUSSION

Plaudits to the dean! Willa Schlesinger saw a problem brewing and sensed the timing was right to resolve it. She also saw a context emerging in which to address some important collateral issues. It cost her valuable time, but she understood very well that if she let it go, it would cost a lot more in the future. The dean was very careful to learn all she could in the time available to her before choosing a path to resolution. In being careful, however, she did not lapse into procrastination.

It should be kept in mind that Dean Schlesinger worked her management of this opportunity into a host of other activities. This is an example of how a dean's life can be interesting and challenging, but can also get out of hand. Without careful setting of priorities and judicious management of the schedule, it can become impossible to find time to tackle situations like this early. Worse yet, it can be all too easy to rationalize the importance of other work because of apprehension about engaging in conflict resolution in a direct and timely way. This is usually the result of lacking the coping skills and perspective setting ability to tackle hard, potentially explosive issues in a timely way. Dean Schlesinger did not suffer from that deficiency.

The dean did not try to go it alone. The university had policy and other resources available to help her address specific aspects of the problems before her. She took advantage of them, but not before making her own assessment of their value. She was required to engage the Office of Affirmative Action, but not Justin Phillips. Before she recruited his services, she looked carefully into his reputation and track record. She was also clear about what problem they would be trying to solve. She very astutely got double duty out of his involvement by engaging him to help coach Darryl Halstead. This was a good idea, even though it did not work out the way they originally intended.

Darryl Halstead revealed a depth of character not evident in his early performance as chair. He stepped down at the end of his second year because he concluded that was the right decision for the department and for him personally. He realized, in part from discussions with Justin Phillips and Dean Schlesinger, that he was not a failure in leaving the chair. Instead, he came to understand that the job did not match his skill set. He would say later, however, that the experience contributed greatly to his eventual election to the presidency of his professional society after long service on its board of directors.

Laura Whitaker took her fate into her own hands. In the long run, she was successful. She pursued her cause in a thoughtful but determined way. She found support from some colleagues and from a key administrator. The effect of seeking resolution of her dilemma was augmented by the wisdom of the dean in placing Laura's circumstances into a larger context. The dean did not allow the situation to become an isolated battle over whether Laura Whitaker was discriminated against. Neither did she allow Laura's situation to become a stalking horse for a further agenda. By following the strategy she developed, the dean filtered the harsh glare of the spotlight on Laura, achieved resolution of her issues, and accomplished a great deal more.

Appendix 4: A Case of Racial Discrimination: Perception or Reality?

Four years into a tenure-track assistant professorship at Eldorado Falls College (EFC), Dr. Michael Washington was losing sleep. Too much pressure was coming from too many directions. An assistant professor of secondary education in the Teachers School, Michael knew all too well the vagaries that could visit one's circumstances, but this burden was becoming more than a reasonable person could be expected to carry.

Eldorado Falls College was in the community of Eldorado Falls, Iowa. Like most college towns in the Midwest, it had a smallish population. And like most such places, Eldorado Falls was mostly white. Of course, Michael knew this from the interview. But he had been so focused on the career opportunity that he had not looked very closely at the community. The people tended toward nice, but standoffish. He could handle that. There was a small African American community that showed signs of growing. A few more black students came to EFC every year, but they were way below being a critical mass. Out of the 2,300 employees at EFC, there were maybe 22 or 23 African American faculty and staff. Mostly staff. The Teachers School had three faculty of color including Michael. The good news was that his church community was very strong. In fact, it was the center of Michael's social world. Eldorado Falls College had one African American full professor. Fremont Adams was the senior member of the black community in

Eldorado Falls and revered by every African American, on campus and off. He held the respect of all whites and was a close friend of many.

What Michael had no way of foreseeing, at least with any certainty or definition, was the merger of Eldorado Falls College with Northwestern State University (NSU). The logic of the merger was long and complicated, but mostly made sense. It had become a reality in Michael's second year. The president of Eldorado Falls College now reported to the president of Northwestern State University. Likewise, the vice president for academic affairs at EFC reported to the provost at NSU. It made sense on paper and, to some extent, on the ground.

The merger presented opportunities, but it also created problems. The one that affected Dr. Washington the most was that the standards for tenure and promotion were being revised—mostly in the direction of more research. The basic idea was that stronger, more research-oriented master's programs at EFC would put them on a more even level with the mother university, Northwestern State. This would allow EFC to serve as a feeder for Northwestern State's Ph.D. programs, which it was struggling to expand. Some young faculty felt that the rules were being changed in the middle of the game. That included Michael Washington.

The faculty in the Teachers School was a pretty good lot, Michael thought. When, after the first six months, he was asked by Fremont Adams how he liked his colleagues, he responded, "OK, I think. I believe they are going to be fine."

Professor Adams pushed it a little. He asked Michael how they treated him. His response was, "Most of them are very nice. They are very respectful, I think." He thought, but did not say, that he could not tell if they liked him or not.

There was one other thing that Dr. Washington had expected, but underestimated. The growing number of African American students coming to EFC created greater awareness of a serious retention problem. To the chagrin of the administration, the five-year retention rate for African American and Hispanic students was less than one-fourth that for white and Asian students. The part-time multicultural affairs office had become full-time. Steve Romero, the new director, was pushing hard for more faculty involvement in engaging African American and Hispanic students. The effort was beginning to show promise, but it took time. Steve worked himself beyond reasonable limits and twisted a lot of arms for help. Michael Washington was on his list. Steve Romero had found Michael to be engaging, easy to talk to, and a terrific role model for black students. In fact, he was a great role model for all students. A handsome man, and engaging by nature, he was articulate and professional. Intuitively, the students knew he liked them.

As a result, Dr. Washington was mentoring a group of eight African American undergraduate students, all but one of whom was in the social sciences. He had recently agreed to be the faculty advisor for the Black Student Association, but just for a year. He knew that would take time, but it was consuming more energy than he had anticipated. People noticed. Recently, the vice president for academic affairs, Ralph Baker, had stopped Michael on campus and thanked him for the good effect he was having. His dean, Nathan Franz, had pointed out in a school meeting how faculty mentoring could boost the success rate of students generally, and students of color in particular. He used Michael Washington as an example of how to do it right. Michael's department head, David Heston, had also mentioned his work with students more than once. It took a lot of time, but Michael felt good about it. Based on what these decision makers were telling him, he thought the college valued him and his efforts.

Now, Michael was finishing his fourth year at EFC. He had his fifth year ahead of him and the up-or-out tenure and promotion decision the following year. His tenure and promotion packet would be due less than 18 months from now. A final decision would follow the subsequent January or February. So, in reality, he had one more academic year in which to prepare.

Michael was now in a meeting with his department head, David Heston. Heston had reviewed Michael's progress and that of one other probationary faculty member, Judith Fountain, with the tenured faculty and was summarizing the feedback. They had discussed Michael's work before, but this was the first time the faculty collectively had scrutinized his progress. The department did not have a formal mid-probationary review process, but there was talk of implementing one since the merger. David Heston had been head for just 18 months. This meeting had started just like any other. But as it evolved, the trajectory was straight downhill. At this point, Heston was quoting and paraphrasing from comments submitted by faculty members about Michael's progress toward tenure.

"Michael is an asset to the department," one faculty member wrote. "I like him personally. His teaching is satisfactory, but not strong. He has been very helpful in mentoring students, especially students of color and at-risk students. However, this is the first time I have seen a compilation of his credentials in several years. I am alarmed that he has made so little progress in scholarship. After four years he has published two papers, and he is third author on one of those. This falls way short of the old college standards, let alone those being discussed."

Another added, "I like Dr. Washington a great deal. However, I am very concerned about him. He has not became engaged in a real way with the academic community."

They continued in a similar vein.

"Michael is very personable. He has done a great deal to improve how we treat students of color, especially those at risk. However, I cannot see evidence of his developing a body of scholarship, even in the context of our mission, which is primarily teaching undergraduates. I think what he does offsets this deficiency, but am afraid that most people won't see it this way."

"While research is not a big deal at EFC, it is getting bigger and Michael is at just about zero in that area. Teaching and related scholarship are our first priority. Michael's work with students is important, but it cannot replace academic basics."

The list went on, but always along the same lines. People liked Dr. Washington personally. Most students loved him. But he was deemed not to be substantively involved in the core of the academic mission. Where some ongoing scholarship would have been sufficient, he appeared to have nothing, or nearly nothing.

Dr. Washington's anxiety showed in his face, which David Heston had learned was like an open book. "David," Michael said, looking out the window, then directly at his boss, "how can this be? We have talked many times. You have never indicated I was not doing what I should. Neither did your predecessor. For that matter, neither has anyone else. I have only one more year to work on these things, and my colleagues are saying that I have nothing."

Heston thought a moment before he spoke. The two were seated in his office, a pleasant little spot on the corner of Milford Hall. Sheer luck had placed Heston in that office years ago, and he had kept it when he became head, even though the departmental secretary was situated down the hall. This room had two windows on the corner with a far better view than the dean enjoyed.

"It's not all bad," he finally said. "They like you personally and recognize the value of your leadership with the students, especially students of color. So do I by the way. I want to be clear, here. In my view, you have been responsible for some real advances in their success. In our school especially."

"Dr. Heston," Michael said, leaning forward over the little conference table, "what about my research? I don't have results at this point, but I do have a solid start and I'm working on a good idea. And, after all, teaching is the main part of our mission."

Heston thought back on the discussion among the faculty about Michael's work. The nature of his research had come up more than once but, oddly enough, it had not appeared on any of the written comments. The gist of the project was that Michael would interview 50 white secondary school teachers, half women and half men, with a standard set of questions about their experience teaching in two different inner-city secondary school environments. He hoped to use the information gleaned from the interviews as the basis for a monograph and the creation of a new upper-division course on teaching and learning in low-income, inner-city environments.

Personally, Heston thought the project had worth. A number of the faculty did not. They believed it would be interesting but of no applicable value because the design of the project created no statistical framework within which to evaluate the results. Heston appreciated it because it might create connections that would become learning opportunities for future students. He also felt the content might have application to a part of the curriculum that he saw as weak.

There was another issue to bring up, and it was an even stickier wicket. Heston picked up the last sheet in the stack of comments from the faculty. It raised a point that had been discussed at length in the meeting. Faculty members had been all over the place in their opinions about it.

"There is one last issue, Michael," Heston continued. "It was discussed a lot in the meeting and opinions ranged all over the place. It has to do with teaching and curriculum. This last set of notes includes a comment that kind of sums up a viewpoint shared by a number of people."

Peering out the bottom layer of his bifocals, Heston read from a handwritten scrawl. "Dr. Washington represents a troubling dilemma that has to do with teaching and learning. His performance in the classroom is satisfactory—some would even suggest that it is good. Certainly he has improved over the last four years. The issue is that Michael seems to depart often and far from the content of the syllabus. We depend on that content in other courses, and sometimes it is evident that students have missed important parts of it, even though they received a good grade. Michael spends a lot of class time getting students involved in discussion, which is great, especially considering the size of his classes. However, I am very much afraid he is not covering the material the students need to learn. I know for a fact that he spends what I view to be far too much time on inner-city racial issues at the cost of not covering material critical to our overall curriculum. I don't have any answers on how this should be addressed. However, I do have real concerns as to whether Dr. Washington can be a team player in achieving the overall goals of our school."

There was a long silence. This was a totally new development. He knew his students, most of whom came from rural and small town backgrounds, were drastically deficient in their understanding of these issues. They had no starting point for even developing a thought process about the related issues. He could help them with that. Over and over again, the basic content around which his courses were structured raised issues relevant to race in public schools.

"What about my student ratings?" Michael asked. "They are consistently good. You have said so yourself."

Heston squirmed a little, his graying eyebrows coming together. He explained that the ratings had also been discussed and everyone knew they were good. The upshot of what had turned into a real debate, though, had two parts. One was that while Michael related very well to students, and that meant students generally as well as those of color, there were other issues. This, of course, was one of the failings of putting too much reliance on student ratings. The students knew they liked Michael and that they were learning what he was trying to teach them. But these points bore little or no relationship to his role in attaining the larger curricular objectives. That was the second part. Were the learning objectives of the Teachers School being properly served in Michael's courses?

"What about my academic freedom?" Michael asked. Heston could see angst building, even anger. He regretted the circumstances of the meeting but felt they had to get these issues squarely on the table. Time was short, a fact that Heston also regretted. He knew that he was, to some extent, accountable for that, even though he had been head only a year and a half.

"It seems to me," Dr. Washington went on, "as if there is a double standard at work here." He scooted back in his chair and folded his arms across his chest. "Faculty who have tenure seem to have unlimited control over what they teach and how they teach it. It is very clear, I think, that is not the case for us tenure-track folks. How many times have you and I both heard members of this faculty talk about their course as if it was a personal possession?"

He had Heston there and David knew it. In fact, that was one issue Heston was extremely concerned about and knew he had to tackle. Maybe Michael Washington's situation was a blessing in disguise. He also knew it would be extremely unfair to let Michael's case become a straw man for the curriculum change and course ownership agenda.

They both had had enough for one sitting. In addition, it was passing noon and Heston had a luncheon commitment. They agreed to get back together two days hence. David Heston left the meeting unsettled. He knew his department's curriculum was far behind events in the field. He had seen this in the most recent accreditation report, now two years old, and confirmed it through his own experience. A majority of the faculty was resistant to change, especially change of the magnitude Heston knew had to come. The merger had resulted in a demand from Northwestern State and the board of curators for EFC to take several significant steps at the institutional level. These included raising the bar in terms of scholarship, strengthening the master's degrees, and creating a much more definitive framework for faculty evaluation, the granting of tenure, and promotion. All of this was going on at once. Michael Washington was caught in the middle. So, for that matter, was David Heston.

For his part, Michael Washington felt confused, angry, betrayed, and afraid. He knew all too well the risk of not being awarded tenure and promotion. At best it would impede his career. At worst it would end it, at least in terms of his aspirations for a life in a college environment. While he was walking to the student union for a burger and Coke, he flipped his cell phone open and dialed the multicultural affairs office for Steve Romero. Steve was out, having lunch with a group of Asian students. About 1:15 Michael's cell phone sounded off with 76 trombones. Steve Romero had seen his number on caller ID and was returning the call. Given that Steve was tied up until 4:00 and Michael was on his way to class, they agreed to meet in Steve's office at 4:30. When Romero asked what the meeting was about, Michael thought a minute and finally said it was too complicated to describe over the phone.

When they eventually closed the door of Steve's office and collapsed into the deep, soft chairs in the corner, both men were about done in. Michael looked around Steve's office, making small talk. Somehow the décor and furniture arrangement created one big comfort zone. A lamp on the small green table between them cast a warm, yellow glow that created a sense of welcome. Michael suspected this was not accidental. It contrasted substantially with the dean's office, which was a display of leather chairs, glass-topped desk, and walnut coffee table. The latter was protected by a power image of an eagle, wings spread, talons extended.

"Nice digs, Steve," Michael said. "Makes you want to settle right in. Don't be offended if I just crash right here in this cushy chair."

Romero considered revealing his secret—his chief consultant in furniture arrangement, accessories, and Feng Shui, one Artesia Romero. He decided to save it for another day. "Thanks," he said. "I like it. Now, what do we need to talk about?"

Michael started at the beginning, meaning the day he first arrived at EFC. He did a thumbnail sketch until he came to this morning's meeting with David Heston. Then he went into more and more detail, and Steve Romero asked more and more questions.

"Does your department not have specific criteria and standards for promotion and tenure?" Steve inquired, fingering the collar of his Hawaiian shirt. "Surely there is some frame of reference that guides these decisions." He realized that this was the first matter of this kind that he had encountered since his arrival. There was a whole lot he needed to learn.

"Not yet," Michael replied. "Northwestern is imposing that requirement, but like most departments at EFC, mine is just now getting into developing them. It is proving to be an extremely contentious exercise."

He paused, wondering how much detail to go into. The potential impact of this project on his own promotion and tenure, albeit indirect, had not hit him until well after his meeting with David Heston. "There is a ferocious debate," he continued, "about criteria and standards. Procedure hasn't even come up yet. It's going to take a while."

"So," Steve remarked after a moment's reflection, "the only standard for the present is the university-wide one, which is kind of boilerplate stuff, like 'have the makings of a national reputation', and so forth." He stroked the corner of his moustache. "That's much too arbitrary for a situation like yours."

It was then that Dr. Washington came to the point that had been dogging him since his meeting with David Heston. He realized now that it had been in the back of his mind for months, maybe years. It was the last thing he wanted to get into, but felt he must. "How do I know," Michael asked, "that all these comments are not based on race, in some subtle way?"

He shifted around in his chair, and Romero could tell Michael was clearly uncomfortable getting into the realm of race. Nonetheless, he pressed ahead. "After all," he continued, "the issues that are being raised have a lot to do with my inclusion of race-related content in my classes. All I am trying to do is give these students some idea about the real issues in racially mixed public schools. It is very obvious the students are dangerously deficient in that area."

Steve Romero had known this would become the central question. He also knew it was very dangerous ground. He did not want to see Michael Washington's tenure become an affirmative action issue. If he was granted tenure and promoted that way, his success would be tainted, through the underground, by the notion that it was an "affirmative action case, not really on the merits." Not only would that hurt Michael Washington, it would hurt the entire effort to advance diversity among the faculty.

They talked at length about these basic questions. Was racial bias a factor in the assessment of Michael Washington's work? Should he not be recognized and rewarded for what he had been encouraged to do, as well as basic teaching and research? Underlying these questions was a more fundamental one, a nuance that whites almost never understood. *If such concerns were valid, would the issue really be race, or would it be cultural differences related to race?* This was not a rhetorical question. Romero knew all too well that Michael Washington, just like Steve Romero, lived a qualitative life in a quantitative environment. Community issues, like mentoring African American students, would be embedded deep in Michael's spirit. They would weigh much more heavily on who he was than lists of grants and publications. The two men talked about this a while. Romero realized that while Michael knew exactly what he was getting at, he had never really thought through the implications of how the two ways of looking at the world would impact his academic career. Six o'clock rolled around. Steve was late for supper, and they had ground the subject as fine as they could, at least for now.

"Before we break up," Romero said, "I need to be very clear on a basic point. I do not handle official complaints, and I have no adjudicatory authority. If, and I think it is a big if, you come to the point of actually making a discrimination complaint, that would go to the Office of Affirmative Action, which has been consolidated on the Northwestern State campus. The good news is that I am able to take the role of advocate in certain situations, without having a conflict of interest. So I wind up being a broker, facilitator, and go-between, all wrapped up in one. How about we think this over for a day or so? I would be happy to talk informally with some people, for example, David Heston, the dean, the vice president."

It was Thursday, so they decided to meet again the following Monday and determine what to do next. Dr. Washington left deeply disturbed and very confused. He was having great difficulty getting his situation in perspective.

Then it was Sunday. Michael attended church, as was his practice. Before leaving home, he called his mother in North Carolina. This was a valued ritual every week. Michael drew much strength from his mother. Beatrice Washington had worked two jobs at a time, helping him earn a bachelors degree from Howard University. His father's early death had left him and his sister and mother in dire straits. They pulled together, though, in every way they could, and today they were closer than ever. Michael's sister Tessa taught biology in a Baltimore high school. She was married to a dentist. They had two kids, great kids. Tessa, with heavy reinforcement from their mother, was leaning hard on Michael to find the right woman. He would make a great husband and father. And his mother loved grandchildren.

Church was nondenominational. The music was terrific. The preaching was powerful, relevant, and profound. The testimonials were inspirational. At the closing, the power of the anthem, "We Shall Overcome," flowed through Michael's spirit like the Jordan through Israel.

This music had attended the civil rights movement from hard-won rhetorical concessions to the beginnings of real hope and the emergence of an embryonic equity. Something else flowed through Michael as the congregation joined hands and sang. That something else was community. These people were there for Michael, as he was for them. They believed in him. His success was important to their collective future, especially the future of their young people. The ethic of the community weighed heavily upon Michael Washington, an ethic of shared hope and shared responsibility.

Monday came. Michael Washington and Steve Romero reconvened and made several decisions. It had come to Romero, by way of a discreet phone call from Fremont Adams himself, that there was a spreading awareness of Michael's situation. Michael, quite naturally, had discussed the matter with him as an elder and a mentor, sitting on the church steps after yesterday's service. At least one other individual, probably more, had put two and two together based on a few indiscreet comments made by concerned members of the secondary education department.

"It would be all too easy," Dr. Fremont had cautioned in his deep, resonant voice, "for this matter to enlarge out of proportion. We feel very strongly about Dr. Washington's outstanding qualities. This issue needs to be addressed quickly and with a great deal of discretion."

Fremont Adams had gone on to say that he and his colleagues in the Black Faculty Caucus, small as it was, stood ready to help in any way. With Dr. Adams permission, Steve Romero recounted this conversation to Michael Washington.

"I have the sense," he later said to Michael, "that you have a pretty good relationship with David Heston. The gentleman has a reputation for being objective. I would suggest that you continue talking this through with him and that I have a conversation with the dean of the Teachers School. I have had some limited dealings with him. He is a good listener and, I think, a straight shooter."

Michael and Steve agreed that this made sense, with one serious question. "I don't want to appear to be going over Dr. Heston's head,"

Michael asserted, "especially without him knowing it. We have to be able to trust each other."

Steve thought this through, alternately massaging the muscle between his left thumb and forefinger, and a spot on the back of his hand. He had a tendency to headaches and had learned long ago that this averted them. He switched the treatment from his left to his right hand. "That's a very good point," he agreed. "Look, Michael, one can never go wrong, at least for long, just laying out the truth. Dr. Heston knows you have good reason to be concerned. It would come as no surprise that you would talk to me, or to the dean for that matter."

Romero paused, thought a moment, and went on. "Just tell him about our conversation. Tell him you want to continue to work together to create a clear framework for your last probationary year. Tell him also that based on our discussion, I am going to talk to your dean. Be clear that I am not complaining about Dr. Heston or even about the situation. I need to articulate the broader concerns your situation raises regarding tenure and retention of faculty of color."

Over the ensuing two weeks, that is what they did. David Heston, to his credit, felt good enough about himself that he was not defensive over Steve Romero talking to the dean. In fact, after another conversation with Michael Washington, he had his own talk with him.

Nathan Franz had been around the bend and back. One reason he had been hired while the merger was in progress, was his strong history in the K–12 system. He had served in small rural schools, mid-sized blue-collar schools, and inner-city environments where poverty and desperation made being a principal, then superintendent, challenging to say the least. Franz had served as chair of a large special education department before coming to EFC. Now in his third year, the dean had hit his stride. He had made several leadership changes, one being the appointment of David Heston.

Franz was an impressive looking man in his early 50s. "David," he was saying, "this matter has the potential to become serious, from several perspectives. First and foremost, it could create an unfair situation for Dr. Washington. Beyond that, it could really hurt our efforts to bring some objectivity to the promotion and tenure process. If Michael's situation is allowed to be politicized, there will be some who argue that social and political values are being imposed on academic principles." The dean leaned back in his chair. "I'm probably missing something," he added.

"Right now," Heston replied, "granting tenure and promotion to Michael would be viewed by some of my faculty as political correctness. If they voted today, I'm afraid a significant majority would vote against him. I would have a very difficult decision to make about my own recommendation. Even though the faculty like him personally and value some of his work, most do not believe it is scholarship."

He thought about what he had just said for a minute. Franz saw his face brighten, as if a very large light bulb came on. "That's it," he went on, leaning in Franz's direction, "I really believe it may be as simple as that. Michael's work with the students is not seen as scholarship. Neither is his divergence from the syllabus."

The dean got it. "In a way," he replied, "what we have here is a convergence of a value system that differs from the standard view most of the faculty hold and the question of what is scholarship."

"So," Heston continued, "let's hold that thought a minute. In my department at least, we have a very pressing need for a major curriculum overhaul. The truth is that much of what Michael digresses to in his teaching is content that should have a much bigger place in our learning objectives. In fact, we don't have real learning objectives. We just have old syllabi."

"All right," Franz responded, "let me raise two further points. Is curriculum design scholarship? And while you are thinking about that, is there an element of research embedded in Michael's work with student mentoring and retention? Are there specific things he can learn, or demonstrate, that can become part of the literature?"

Their plate was getting pretty full. The two men sat for a moment, trying to get their minds around all these questions. Franz tapped a little rhythm on the edge of his table with a ballpoint pen. Heston scratched his chin with the end of his little finger.

"I would like to add one more, broader point," Franz said at length. He kept thinking about a conversation he had recently with Steve Romero. "African American and Hispanic communities and, to some extent, women, have a different view of the world than faculty assessing Michael for tenure," he went on. "Steve Romero came to see me a few days ago. I think you know that. He really set me to thinking. One of the things going on here is that Michael Washington and the African American community have a much more qualitative, community-based perspective than the publication-counting, grant-totaling view of most white faculty members."

Franz paused to frame his thoughts. "That point is fundamental, I would guess, to many of the retention problems we have with students and, for that matter, faculty of color. Is there a way to gain some synergy between the two perspectives, these two worldviews, and address these other questions at the same time?"

Nathan and David both had started making notes. This was an urgent, teachable moment. They were scribbling ideas from the last 10 minutes, comparing their thoughts aloud. Shortly, they both had the same list:

- What is scholarship? Review Boyer's Book, *Scholarship* something or other.

- Can a mentoring program be developed into a body of scholarship?

- Should not people be evaluated against what they have been encouraged to do?

- Is it possible to develop criteria for evaluating service, similar to research and teaching? It seems very difficult. If so, can anything about service be thought of as scholarship?

- Can curricular reform and design be viewed as scholarship? If so, how does one assess its value?

- Is there a way to leverage the different worldviews held by minority and majority faculty? Can these issues be built into a major effort to overhaul the curriculum?

- Can such questions be addressed in our efforts to create criteria and standards for evaluation, promotion, and tenure in this college?

- Can these issues be successfully engaged if everyone in a department has the same basic expectations of productivity, or is there a need for greater flexibility in pathways to success (tenure and promotion)?

Heston and Franz thought they had taken it as far as they could. They each kept a copy of their notes. Franz committed to put this on his next administrative council agenda. As they went on to their separate appointments, both realized that while they had some very good thinking in hand, much of it would be controversial and all of it would take time. If they were not careful, Michael Washington could wind up in a crossfire. The more he thought about it, the more Nathan Franz reckoned he had better walk through all of this with Vice President Baker. The last thing he wanted was to get out on a limb without being sure where Ralph was.

Ralph, as it turned out, got it. In fact, he already had it. One reason was his own emerging understanding of some of the related issues facing EFC. The other was that Fremont Adams had beaten the dean to the punch and met with Baker for two hours the day before.

Dean Franz handed the vice president a copy of his list—which he had cleaned up a little since the brainstorming session with David Heston. Baker scanned it and said with an understated little smile, "This is very good stuff, Nathan. Are you sure Fremont Adams didn't write it for you? Or maybe Steve Romero?"

They both could see Fremont's fingerprints on the whole scenario, with a few superimposed by Steve Romero. But what the heck? Like Ralph said, it was very good stuff. They talked for a long time about each point. Baker had copies of Boyer's classic *Scholarship Reconsidered: The Priorities of the Professoriate*, which Nathan had read, and the follow up by Charles Glassick and his colleagues, *Scholarship Assessed: Evaluation of the Professoriate,* which he had not. Baker knew when to seize the moment. He told Franz he was going to put this on the agenda of the council of academic deans, if it was all right with him, because everyone ought to be thinking about this stuff. Nathan said that was fine. In fact, he would benefit from the reaction of the other deans.

Baker knew he had a great summary of a very complicated set of issues in his hands and, equally important, he had an ally, Nathan Franz. He had wanted to get his teeth into this for a long time. Fremont Adams had created a sense of urgency as only Fremont could. Adams had been careful to stress many times that his objective was not to plead Michael Washington's case, but to take in hand the issues it raised and see to it the college and, if need be, Northwestern State, addressed them in a constructive way. He had not been accompanied by his colleagues in the Black Faculty Caucus, but invited Baker to meet with them, which he agreed to do. In fact, Baker offered to tap his foundation account to buy lunch, which Adams thought was a grand idea.

What Baker did not tell Dean Franz, at least for now, was that Steve Romero also had come to see him. The difference was that Steve talked about Michael Washington specifically, rather than all these other issues. In his soft-spoken, articulate way, Steve had pointed out some very cogent aspects. Michael Washington had been doing what he had been encouraged to do. Now, when his career was on the line, he was being evaluated on different criteria. He had accomplished miracles with students of color, especially at-risk African American students, some of whom viewed him as their lifeline to EFC. Washington's case represented issues important to recruitment and retention of faculty of color institution wide. Michael's department had no stated criteria or standards against which to evaluate his work, so how could there be assurance against arbitrary and capricious action? Finally, the meeting which produced the alarming feedback was the first time the faculty in the Department of Elementary Education had been asked, collectively, to evaluate Washington's progress, and at a very late date indeed in his probationary appointment. Thank goodness David Heston had the presence of mind to solicit their views this spring instead of a year from now. Romero had made it clear that he had come to discuss this without portfolio; neither Washington nor anyone else knew about it. His purpose was to better prepare the vice president to deal constructively with what could become a very explosive situation. Ralph agreed that could happen. Being a man who liked to get his thoughts together, he kept his own council about the Romero visit.

The thing that crystallized in Dean Franz's mind on his way back to his office was that he and David Heston had to separate Michael Washington's situation from all the issues it raised, which he was now more determined than ever to pursue. Parallel to his efforts at the college level, David Heston would also have to bring greater definition to the issues in his department. That would apply in different ways to Michael Washington and to the tenured secondary education faculty. Candor would be essential. Clear goals based on criteria and standards that the rest of the faculty took some ownership in must be established quickly, with a view to Washington's last full probationary year. Ditto for Judith Fountain. If the dean needed to involve himself in that goal-setting process, he would do so. The merger of the issues raised in his meeting with David Heston and the ongoing efforts by the other departments in his school to develop unit-level criteria and standards for evaluation, promotion, and tenure would be led by Franz.

On balance, it worked pretty well, but not exactly according to plan. David Heston had a series of meetings with his tenured faculty on the one hand and with Michael Washington on the other. The concerns of the faculty were defined in succinct terms that could be addressed through specific goals created in concert with Michael Washington. It was acknowledged that the change in departmental leadership had put Michael at a disadvantage. It was also acknowledged that this had been exacerbated by people in authority encouraging and recognizing him for a lot of work that the faculty per se did not believe was fundamental to their mission. The inherent unfairness was self-evident. However, it was also agreed among the faculty, Heston, and Washington that two things must be considered fundamental. One was that Washington must demonstrate that he was covering material in his courses that other faculty depended on in theirs. Most conceded that curriculum revision was essential. Heston initiated a new approach to curriculum development in the department. First, he disbanded the existing curriculum committee. He had come to realize that they had the biggest stake in the status quo. Then he appointed a small task force to create a new set of learning objectives. The group included one person from each of the other departments in the school. This was controversial, but the results were exciting, so people got over it.

Eighteen months later, Michael Washington was granted tenure and promoted to associate professor, but it was not smooth sailing. Even with all the work that went into the last year, the faculty in his department were split. David Heston supported him, noting that by traditional EFC college-wide standards, his candidacy was marginal but that he had proven ability in areas that were emerging as vital to better preparation of K–12 teachers. The dean's advisory group on promotion and tenure opposed his candidacy by a margin of one. The dean supported him. At the end of the day, Ralph Baker did also.

The issues surrounding scholarship proved too big for one school to tackle by itself. However, by the middle of the year, Ralph Baker and Nathan Franz had all but one of the others deans fired up. In the spring, the vice president appointed a task force with the charge to make recommendations on a working definition of scholarship for the next generation of scholars at EFC, and to create example criteria and standards against which it might be evaluated. The dean of arts and sciences chaired the task force, which included Michael Washington and Steve Romero along with some of the most potent scholars in the institution. The project took 18 months and included more than one knock down, drag out donnybrook. One thing everyone agreed on after the first month, however, was that scholarship and research would no longer be used interchangeably in whatever policy the group would finally recommend.

In parallel to the goings on in the task force, David Heston never stopped pressing questions on his faculty. There were preparing for the time when they could work within an institution-wide framework to finalize a new, truly forward-looking document to guide future decisions about rewarding faculty work. At the epicenter of the effort, this question slowly formed: Is the mission of the department truly confined to teaching, research, and service, or does it include mentoring, role modeling, and constituent building?

DISCUSSION

If Eldorado Falls College had had department-level criteria, standards, and procedures for annual evaluation, promotion, and tenure in place, Michael Washington's situation might not have developed. A mandatory mid-probationary review policy would have had a salutary effect. The very act of creating such policies and updating them periodically engages people and tends to create a collaborative understanding about collective goals. Surprises late in the probationary period are always a major source of conflict.

The transition from one department head to another was a two-edged sword. On the one hand, it probably contributed to a period of confusion and lost continuity. However, it also resulted in bringing a perceptive, committed problem solver into the picture, in the person of David Heston.

The people involved had the right kind of motivation. They wanted the best for the institution and the individuals in it, understanding that if their institution did well, they as administrators would also. This was a good example of managing like basketball (see Chapter 9). This philosophy can only work if everyone plays as a team. There was a lot of passing the ball back and forth to get down the floor. Getting the ball to the right person at the right time was critical. It should be kept in mind that the team was pretty broad and diverse. It included Nathan Franz, David Heston, Ralph Baker, Steve Romero, and Fremont Adams. In a sense it included Michael Washington also. He threw the ball in bounds and became a player as events transpired. At one point, Steve Romero took the ball and dribbled down the baseline for a lay up in his private meeting with Ralph Baker.

This case could easily have erupted into a racial incident, most likely as an affirmative action claim, followed by a grievance and possibly a lawsuit. Such outcomes would have generated a great deal of campus-wide angst. Such a turn of events would have set the Teachers School, and probably the entire college, back in everything they were trying to do. It certainly would have caused their much-needed efforts to create a more helpful framework for annual evaluation, promotion, and tenure decisions to be labeled as racially motivated. It would have damaged efforts to enhance the recruitment and retention of faculty, staff, and students of color. Specifically, it would have damaged Michael Washington's career, perhaps permanently. However, because people worked together, motivated by the collective best interest of the institution rather than by individual agendas, the incident became a vehicle through which to do the right thing in the Washington case and further the institution in important areas at the same time.

A key element in turning an impending furor into a positive event was getting past race to the cultural issues attendant to race. Rhetorical exercises like "keep the playing field level," "we need a faculty that looks like the real world," and so forth create very limited possibilities. Only when the institution seeks to find synergy between the cultural strengths of the various ethnicities and both genders can it make real progress. This means the kind of progress that can advance the institution, both culturally and academically. The people attending the Washington matter began to understand this and act accordingly.

Suggested Readings

Bowling, D., & Hoffman, D. (Eds.). (2003). *Bringing peace into the room: How the personal qualities of the mediator impact the process of conflict resolution.* San Francisco, CA: Jossey-Bass.

Brevitz, K. F. (2003, May/June). Legal resources for higher education administrators and faculty. *Change, 35*(3), 55–59.

Cheldelin, S. I., & Lucas, A. F. (2003). *Academic administrator's guide to conflict resolution.* San Francisco, CA: Jossey-Bass.

Deutsch, M., & Coleman, P. T. (Eds.). (2000). *The handbook of conflict resolution: Theory and practice.* San Francisco, CA: Jossey-Bass.

Diamond, R. M. (2004). *Preparing for promotion, tenure, and annual review: A faculty guide* (2nd ed.). Bolton, MA: Anker.

Fisher, R., Ury, W., & Patton, B. (1997). *Getting to yes: Negotiating agreement without giving in* (3rd ed.). New York, NY: Penguin.

Fuller, J. W. (Ed.). (1983). *New directions in higher education: No. 41. Issues in faculty personnel policies.* San Francisco, CA: Jossey-Bass.

Furlong, G. (2005). *Conflict resolution toolbox: Models and maps for analyzing, diagnosing, and resolving conflict.* San Francisco, CA: Jossey-Bass.

Higgerson, M. L. (1996). *Communication skills for department chairs.* Bolton, MA: Anker.

Higgerson, M. L., & Rehwaldt, S. S. (1993). *Complexities of higher education administration.* Bolton, MA: Anker.

Holton, S. A. (Ed.). (1995). *New directions in higher education: No. 92. Conflict management in higher education.* San Francisco, CA: Jossey-Bass.

Holton, S. A. (1998). *Mending the cracks in the ivory tower: Strategies for conflict management in higher education.* Bolton, MA: Anker.

Landau, S., Landau, B., & Landau, D. (2001). *From conflict to creativity: How resolving workplace disagreements can inspire innovation and productivity.* San Francisco, CA: Jossey-Bass.

Mallory, B. L., & Thomas, N. L. (2003, September/October). When the medium is the message: Promoting ethical action through democratic dialogue. *Change, 35*(5), 10.

Mayer, B. (2000). *The dynamics of conflict resolution: A practitioner's guide.* San Francisco, CA: Jossey-Bass.

McCarthy, J., Ladimer, I., & Sirefman, J. P. (1984). *Managing faculty disputes.* San Francisco, CA: Jossey-Bass.

Moore, C. W. (2003). *The mediation process: Practical strategies for resolving conflict* (3rd ed. rev.). San Francisco, CA: Jossey-Bass.

Ostrander, K. H. (1981). *A grievance arbitration guide for educators.* Boston, MA: Allyn and Bacon.

Seldin, P., & Higgerson, M. L. (2002). *The administrative portfolio: A practical guide to improved administrative performance and personnel decisions.* Bolton, MA: Anker.

Timpson, W. M., Canetto, S. S., Borrayo, E. A., & Yang, R. (Eds.). (2003). *Teaching diversity: Challenges and complexities, identities and integrity.* Madison WI: Atwood.

◆ BIBLIOGRAPHY

Allred, K. (2000). Anger and retaliation in conflict: The role of attribution. In M. Deutsch & P. T. Coleman (Eds.), *The handbook of conflict resolution: Theory and practice* (pp. 236–255). San Francisco, CA: Jossey-Bass.

Boyer, E. L. (1990). *Scholarship reconsidered: Priorities of the professoriate*. Princeton, NJ: Carnegie Foundation for the Advancement of Teaching.

Glassick, C. E., Huber, M. T., & Maeroff, G. I. (1997). *Scholarship assessed: Evaluation of the professoriate*. San Francisco, CA: Jossey-Bass.

Kanter, R. M. (1978). *The changing shape of work: Psychosocial trends in America*. Washington, DC: American Association for Higher Education.

Leaming, D. R. (1998). *Academic leadership: A practical guide to chairing the department*. Bolton, MA: Anker.

INDEX

Communication, xvii
Community
   African American, 92, 191, 205
   ethic, 202
   Hispanic, 92
   principles of, 112
Confidentiality, 39
Conflict and disputes, 1
   about ideas, 1, 4, 5
   about people 2, 4, 5
   and academic environment, 13
   action and reaction, 20
   anger and escalation, 124
   courage in, 7
   fiscal impact, 3
   gender, 24
   intractable, 147
   policy development, 47
   prevention, resolution, and management,
      109
   productive, 4
   race, 24
   resolution, methods of, 27
   responsibility for, 118
   unproductive, 1, 15
Core values, 109, 111
   qualitative versus quantitative, 92, 200
Counseling and coaching, 29, 102, 116
   confidentiality, 104
   executive coach, 102
   human systems consultants, 102
   group dynamics and, 103
Curmudgeon, xv, 23

Darwin, 2
Deans, 74
   culture and style, 74
Department heads, chairs, 14, 76, 114, 117,
   135
   appointed versus rotating, 75, 76
   effectiveness, 14
   faculty careers, 77
   managing debate and conflict, 77
   orientation and training, 73, 119, 131

Discrimination, xviii, 24, 54, 183
   gender, 54, 83, 110
   gender bias, 169, 176
   legal standard, 25, 117
   racial, 45, 54, 110, 191

Education, 119, 131
Emotion, 20, 124
Entry and exit, 117
   multiple points of, 117
Evaluation, xvi, 42,
   of administrators, 131
   annual, 49, 110, 133
   mid-probationary review and, 49, 130
   of service, 205
   tenure, promotion, and, 49, 130

Facilitation, 29, 117
   human systems consultants, 102
Fact-finding, xii, 21, 34, 121
   framing and reframing, 22, 34, 41, 45,
      141, 182
   and perspective setting, 21
   truth and fairness, 70
Faculty (university) handbook, xiii, 42
   as a contract, xiii
Fairness, 70
   fact-finding and truth, 70
   stakeholders, 70, 121
Fear, 124

Glassick, C. E., 58, 207
Governance, xv, xvi, 13, 61
   administration, xvi, 61
   board, xv, 61, 113
   conflict and, 2
   faculty, xv, 18
   faculty senate, 14, 19, 159, 164
   policy development, 55
Grievance, xviii, 36, 37, 43, 52
   as a form of arbitration, 43

Harassment, xviii, 110
   legal standard, 86